What People ~~~ ~~~
Counterc~~~~~~~~~~ ~~~~~~~~~~

"In *Countercultural Parenting*, Lee Nienhuis offers a paradigm shift desperately needed in today's culture. She reminds us that the journey to raising children with character begins with us! Lee writes that we have to personally and actively cultivate a deep life of virtue and moral fiber, relying on God's power to produce the fruit of the Spirit in our lives as we live out our faith and train up our kids. This refreshing book is filled with transparent stories and biblical advice to help you trust God with your children's future."

John Fuller, vice president of Audio
and cohost of the *Focus on the Family* radio program

"Don't think you can make a difference in this world? Think again. Your best contribution is to parent with countercultural intentionality. The words in this book will show you how."

Jill Savage, author of *Real Moms...Real Jesus*

"Do you need to believe you can parent well in hard times? Really believe? This is the book for you. You'll find the encouragement and inspiration you need because of Lee's use of Scripture, stories, and specific ideas. She teaches us how to join the oppositional forces that trigger cultural changes and how to make sure our kids are in this group. Lee both inspired me *and* equipped me. We can battle and win!"

Kathy Koch, PhD, founder and president of Celebrate Kids, Inc.,
cofounder of Ignite the Family, and author of *Start with the Heart*

"Are you stunned by the corruption, foolishness, and egomania displayed by our leaders and celebrated in our culture? Are you devastated by the reverberating character deficits you see in your own kids—and even in yourself? With wisdom, wit, and mom-in-the-trenches perspective, Lee leads us to our only character-renovating hope: God and the truth of His Word. Come leave your apathy and hand-wringing behind and follow Lee on a charge to change the world—one mom and kid at a time."

Shannon Popkin, author of *Comparison Girl*

"'For such a time as this' God has placed your child in this world and into your home to fulfill the incredible calling He has for him or her. God knew this period of time would be filled with all sorts of temptations and distractions. Lee's book is masterful in helping parents see and understand that they can raise up children with godly character, morals, values, and strength no matter the child, situation, culture, or parent. This deep, rich resource along with the Bible will help you and your child become remarkable men or women of God!"

Sally Burke, president, Moms in Prayer International

"In our current culture, it's tempting to become lax and disheartened when it comes to matters of character. Thankfully, Lee Nienhuis has diligently and boldly laid out a guidebook to reorient parents with their God-given responsibility to raise children who live under His authority and do some earthly good. I stand with Lee in believing that revival is possible in this generation and the next, beginning with a subgroup who is willing to go against the status quo and train their kids in the countercultural ways of Christ."

Katie M. Reid, author of *Made Like Martha*, cohost of *The Martha & Mary Show*, and mother of five

"As a parent, you have one of life's most precious and holy responsibilities: to shape the character and heart of your children. I'm thankful my friend Lee has poured her heart and soul into these pages for you to have all you need to build on the foundation of faith in your family. Don't get so caught up in the busyness of daily life that you forget to think about the legacy you are instilling every day in your kids. If we want to change the world, we need to start in our homes."

Matt Brown, evangelist, author, and founder of Think Eternity

Counter Cultural Parenting

Lee Nienhuis

HARVEST HOUSE PUBLISHERS
EUGENE, OREGON

Cover design by Studio Gearbox

Interior design by KUHN Design Group

Cover photo © ozzichka, Naoki Kim / Shutterstock

Countercultural Parenting
Copyright © 2020 by Lee Nienhuis
Published by Harvest House Publishers
Eugene, Oregon 97408
www.harvesthousepublishers.com

ISBN 978-0-7369-7823-1 (pbk.)
ISBN 978-0-7369-7824-8 (eBook)

Library of Congress Control Number: 2020932615

Printed in the United States of America

20 21 22 23 24 25 26 27 28 / BP-SK / 10 9 8 7 6 5 4 3 2 1

———————————

For Brendan

The day you were born changed everything.
The world gained a gentleman,
a man of integrity and character.
May it also grow to know you as a man of unshakable faith.

You don't have to be perfect, Son.
There will always be *grace enough* for us both.
I love you forever,
Mom

Now I commit you to God and to the word of his
grace, which can build you up and give you an
inheritance among all those who are sanctified.

ACTS 20:32

Contents

Is It Possible to Raise a Child of Character?

Some authors are called to write books with the advantage of looking back through the rearview mirror. God has not awarded me that luxury. At the time of publication, I will have one kid in high school, two in middle school, and one finishing elementary. By God's grace alone, I have already penned one book. *Brave Moms, Brave Kids: A Battle Plan for Raising Heroes* came from a desperate desire to find a way through the fear that is paralyzing a generation of mothers, myself included. When fear pressed in on me and there was no solution in sight, I found one source of strength, hope, and wisdom: the fact that while I don't know how to do this, God does.

God has parented in every generation, knows what lies ahead, and promises to be with us. Furthermore, He has not failed in one of His promises, and He will not ruin that track record with us. He can be trusted. Though we have not seen a day like this, the Ancient of Days has, and He alone knows the way through it. I believe God's Word contains everything we and our kids need for life, godliness, and faith in our generation (2 Peter 1:3).

The story behind this book is not unlike that of the one before it. *Countercultural Parenting* began as a question to the Lord and has become a manifesto I must declare to the world. It all began the morning after a presidential election—before my eyes opened, before coffee, and before I knew who had been elected. I lay in bed, sighed, and began to pray. "Lord, I don't know who was just elected to serve our nation, but I know we have gone horribly astray." Months of toxic election chatter and revelations had exposed one thing for certain in my mind: We were a nation whose values, priorities, and agendas no longer demanded that a person of noble character lead us.

"Father, are we too far gone? Is it even possible to raise a child to 'act justly and to love mercy and to walk humbly' before You all his days?[1] Are we past the place where our culture would choose *righteousness*?"

In the dark of that early morning, I wrestled with what I feared was the answer to that question. Until three simple words formed in my heart.

Raise that child.

This is my anthem, and it is also yours.

Our Character Is Cracking

We are in a time of revelation and reckoning, a character crisis of epic proportions. The symptoms are evident as we open our curtains and the news apps on our phones. The effects drip from our social media engagement, follow us into the voting booth, and trend in polls. "Cheat. Bribe. Lie." a headline reads.[2] Another claims, "Lies Behind the Laughter, the Truth about America's Dad."[3] My stomach churns. Corruption, coercion, and counterfeit living are commonplace, and it is making the job of raising virtuous children seem like a far-fetched ideal. Truth be told, most days just reading the news makes me feel like I swam in a cesspool. Our headlines are heart ripping, but it is the daily reality of living those headlines that makes us ache.

Our family lives in rural, small-town America, largely protected from crime and scandal, but the disintegration of wholesome values has rolled down our gravel roads as well. Today, our schools address issues like teen vaping, athletes doping, and the recreational use of legalized marijuana. This one-stoplight community deals with embezzlement, greed, prejudice, and abuse of power by authorities. While there is no "wrong side of the railroad tracks," the dividing line between wealth and poverty is painfully obvious, and we live with a constant awareness that children who go to school with ours do not have enough to eat and are shivering in the cold of a Michigan winter.

It's appalling to listen to the morning news, so just forget about primetime television. We can't point to any of our leaders as examples or hold them in honor for fear of what will be revealed tomorrow. Political language today is so hateful, so filled with vitriol, and so lewd that we dare not listen with our kids in the room. This skepticism of authority transfers across the screens and affects the way we view leaders in our towns.

The crashing moral tide and character crisis has also hit the church in gut-wrenching ways. Meant to be a beacon of light to a lost and hurting world, the church is facing its own reckoning. What began in the last decade with the Catholic Church indicted for covering priests' sexual abuse of children has now cascaded like the fall of dominoes as one ministry leader after another is caught in affairs, abuse, and gross immorality. Pastoral pay stubs point to the building of personal empires rather than the body of Christ, and perhaps even more grievous is the disavowing of faith and biblical principles. Yesterday I tossed a book in the trash because I can't stomach reading something written by a Christian who has lived a life of duplicity.

This sifting of our church, culture, and character isn't all bad. With two simple words, an undercurrent of abuse and immorality was exposed, rocking America: "Me too." On October 15, 2017, an actress tweeted a simple message: "If you've been sexually harassed or assaulted write 'me too' as a reply to this tweet."[4] By the next morning, the landscape of our culture had changed as thousands of women responded with the simple hashtag #MeToo. The deafening crack in the silence about the issue of sexual harassment and assault would reverberate around the world as the spotlight began to shine on an issue often swept under the rug.

As the devastating, daily revelations of sexual harassment continued, a new movement, #ChurchToo, turned the spotlight onto perpetrators lurking in the church of Christ. It has been difficult to lift our heads as the church has rightfully faced scrutiny for shaming and silencing victims and as reports of indiscretion and abuse of power by many church leaders have surfaced. Although this immorality may not have happened in the halls of your church or my church in particular, any association with the name of Christ has been tainted.

The cracks in our morality are also manifesting in our kids. Students are showing an increased lack of respect for authority, and schools are powerless to stop it. An environment of fear has emerged, with teachers afraid of crossing parents. I attended 18 different teacher-parent conferences last year, and at one such meeting I was eager to clear up some issues one of my girls was having with her peers. The teacher hung his head and said, "This class is out of control. I'm often sending kids to the office for being disrespectful toward me and each other. I've called parents, only to be told that they don't believe their child is a problem."

I sat in my chair, stunned, because I come from a time when trouble at school meant double trouble when you got home. Again and again I have been told that teaching has changed, that the needs are different, and that teachers are forced to spend more time on behavior management than on teaching.

Bullying, both in school and on social media, plagues our kids. No wonder there has been a critical rise in depression, anxiety, pornography, and drug consumption among our children. The trends are staggering and costly, and we can only wonder when we will reach the breaking point.

Is it crazy to imagine that we could raise children who are godly, who will grow into righteous leaders? Could they become men and women who choose from the earliest age to be people of character, steadfast and immovable? Are we too far gone?

Friend, because people lack a strong, noble character, our world lacks stability. But what if our one great contribution to this world was to raise godly children who could bring stability and strength? What if, by working together, we could rebuild the broken-down walls of our nation, our churches, and our world? What if we could raise our children in a countercultural way, back on the righteous path that God can bless?

The New Question

One morning I woke up and asked the Lord if it was even possible to find a person of character, a person who lived righteously. Could my children live free from the love of money and the corruption that inevitably comes from prioritizing pleasure, power, and popularity? Could my daughters and sons choose righteousness and sexual purity in an age of perversion? How could I, as a mother, raise a child of character who would follow the Lord, serve others, and spend his or her days on the pursuit of heaven coming to earth through Christ?

"Lord, is it possible?"

What you hold in your hands today is the answer to the prayer that followed my question: *Show me.*

Is it possible to raise a child of character, one who will reflect Christ to the world—not by their religious affiliation but by the depth of their conformity to the image of God's Son? By God's grace and with His help, I say, "Yes."

However, it will be a costly journey for parent and child. The moral tide of our culture is sweeping virtue, hard work, integrity, and godliness out to sea, and the effort to raise a child with steadfast character will most certainly be countercultural. Raising a child of character will require constant attention, heavenly perspective, and endurance that we can scarcely imagine on this side of eternity.

As I have prayed to understand the substance of character and how to cultivate it, I have had to lay aside my pride. We have not reached this scary place in our culture because of a faceless "them." We have reached this scary place because of *us*. It is easy to pin the blame on a perverse population, sensationalism in the media, or Christian celebrities gone awry, but the Spirit continually presses this one driving truth on my heart: There will be no character cleanup in our nation or in the body of Christ until I grapple with me, my sin, and my own failings. It is time to own my role in this mess and begin addressing sin within the walls of my own home. Society is merely a barometer of a large group of homes, and the work of rebuilding can start in mine.

These are the lessons and stories—biblical, historical, and personal—that are shaping my understanding. I once again choose to publicly lay aside my fear and to believe the God who will faithfully keep His own.

His Word and Spirit are our only guides.

For the pleasure of the Lord and
the future of our children,

Lee

1

A Distinguished Character

A Battle for the Hearts of Our Children

> Reputation is what men and women think of us;
> character is what God and angels know of us.
> ATTRIBUTED TO THOMAS PAINE

I sighed as the truth hit me: *My* child has a character problem.

This realization came out of left field and blindsided us. One minute I was putting on makeup and getting ready for a day of vacation with my family, and the next I was holding my child's cell phone, pained by what we had just found. I'm so glad my husband, Mike, had practiced his "I'm not surprised" face, because I had to turn away to mask my feelings of betrayal, confusion, and horror. My mind spun. *My son would never make this choice. He knows better.* While Mike worked through the initial moments with a gentleness that must have come from the Holy Spirit, I reeled.

Mike held our son as he began to unwind. Months of shame were working their way to the surface, and I could hear sobs in the next room. "I'm so sorry. I'm so sorry." I fought for composure.

If I could visit myself in that shell-shocked moment, I would whisper three things in my ear:

One, thank God that your child has been caught. This devastating moment is a gift to him and you. There can be no healing, no repair, and no restoration until the light of truth pierces the darkness, the secrecy, and the shame that has gripped his soul.

Two, this is the perfect time to unwind your identity from that of your children. Setting your hopes on them is too great a burden for them. Drawing affirmation from their positive choices and devastation from their poor choices is unhealthy and unhelpful.

Third and finally, this would be a good time to gather the family and say, "This is an us *problem."*

We all have a character problem. *I* have a character problem. This character problem is systemic and noxious, and our society is ripping at the seams because of it. At the surface, it appears to be a problem that begins and ends with personal failings, but underneath is a battle for the hearts of our children. This isn't simply a moral issue; what we are experiencing is a full-on tactical assault by the enemy of our souls for the lives and future of our families.

It is high time we, as parents, wake up and fight.

Brokenness in Our Midst

This morning a young man crossed the street in front of my van on the way to school. His fancy headphones were draped around his neck, and as he crossed with a bit of a swagger, our eyes met. I took in his changing face and frame.

Connor and my son, Brendan, grew up together. They sat at the same preschool table, learning how to hold chubby pencils and write their names in big block letters. Connor taught my son how to snap his fingers when they were five. They played more innings of baseball together than any of us would care to count. They were friends, and so it did not surprise me at all when Connor lifted his eyes in my direction and recognition flickered in them. Only this time, he didn't raise his hand in my direction for a wave. He is rapidly closing in on high school graduation, and I was lucky that his chin tilted up at me in a cool "Hey."

My window was closed and I was in my pajama pants, but I wanted to jump out of the car and wrap up that big man-child in a hug. Brendan had recently reported that Connor got into trouble in school again, is hanging out with the wrong kids, and is headed in the direction of trouble. I see it too.

I kept driving with a small wave, but as I sit here now, I wonder. What shifted inside of Connor? Is anyone talking to him about the path he is on and where this mess leads—and should it be me who talks to him? What does it say about me if I, loving that boy the way I do, let him fall into the ditch? What does the Lord want from me here, and is that kid my responsibility too?

I don't have the answer for this question, but I can tell you that I drive the same path to school every day, down the same road of our one-stoplight town. I see the same kids growing each day. The mom who used to walk her three well-mannered, well-groomed boys to school has seen one graduate, and the other two walk themselves to school now. The blended family with the gaggle of kids broke up sometime in the spring. Their home is vacant, and I wonder how they are getting on and where they are. I wonder how the kids are doing while their parents take care of their own mess.

What could God do with a generation of parents set on doing the deep and steady work of instilling good character into their children? What might happen if a generation chose to love God with all their heart, mind, soul, and strength and to love their neighbors as they love themselves? What would happen to our nation and world if we wrapped our arms around the next generation and showed them a way of living that was vastly different and better than the direction in which they are currently headed? What if my children and yours were the catalyst God used to change the trajectory of this generation and the next?

I desperately want to find out what would happen if we collectively went all in for the sake of the gospel and our kids, and I'm deeply committed to doing the hard and gritty character work inside me and them.

No Reason but God

The men had conspired long into the night. Daniel was a thorn in their side, and they would do whatever it took to get rid of him. God's favor for him was clear, the king was enamored with him—and if they didn't make a move, it would be too late. The kingdom would be handed over to a foreigner.

This wasn't a game. Daniel's political enemies were real, and they were plotting to kill him.

When I heard this story of Daniel in the past, I imagined a fair-haired young man, maybe in his early twenties. As I recall, the flannelgraph characters used during Sunday school lessons made him look tanned and trim, bright-eyed and strong—you know, the datable kind of guy. I certainly did not picture that, at the point in Daniel's life when he was thrown into the lion's den, he would have been in his eighties. The reality is that his hair—if he had any at all—would have been silver, his skin covered in age spots, and his face lined with years.

By the time we reach the account in Daniel 6, Daniel has served a foreign empire in a key leadership position for about 70 years. He had been taken from his home preceding the fall of Jerusalem as a bright, young teenager with his whole life ahead of him. He was a Jew of noble birth, full of promise, who was ripped from the only home he had known and carried to the palace of Nebuchadnezzar. The Babylonians had swept through Israel, imposing the consequence of Israel's disobedience to God. Jerusalem's noble youth had been carried off to be indoctrinated in the way of the Babylonians.

Upon arrival, the kids were given new names in an effort to strip away their heritage, the memory of their homeland, and the God they had worshipped. Their first true test looked more like a good buffet spread with delicious food and wine than a dangerous first step toward moral decline. To the outsider it would certainly not be seen as a spiritual barometer for how these boys' faith would fare in a foreign, secular land. But that's exactly how the first chapter of the book of Daniel describes these kids' first days in Babylon.

Daniel, surrounded by other Jewish young men, made a decision that the God of his youth in Jerusalem was still his master in Babylon and that the Lord's guidelines for living were still to be obeyed. "Daniel resolved not to defile himself with the royal food and wine…God had caused the official to show favor and compassion to Daniel" (Daniel 1:8-9).

This small choice as a teen set a trajectory of obedience and integrity that would define Daniel for the rest of his life. Not only did he choose obedience to God, but God rewarded that obedience with His favor and poured His blessing upon him. When Daniel's time came to stand before the king of Babylon, he and his three close friends were found to be ten times wiser than the wisest men in the king's service (verse 20).

Integrity leads to blessing. In moments when no one else would make the choice to obey, when it may not even seem wise or could lead to lasting negative consequences, people with integrity believe that God knows what He is doing when He sets boundaries on our lives. Integrity says, "God's way is the best way, come what may," and it believes that there will be a reward for their hidden choices of obedience when no one else cares or applauds.

While the diet selection may have been Daniel's inaugural test, it certainly would not be his last. He was appointed as a key adviser to King Nebuchadnezzar. Daniel, a foreigner, was brought into a sacred place of trust in the kingdom of Babylon, in service to a king who had separated Daniel from his family and could very well have orchestrated their deaths. But Daniel was not a man of vengeance; he was a man of prudence and discretion (Daniel 2:14), a man of prayer (verse 18), and a man of humility (verse 30). Over the years of King Nebuchadnezzar's reign, Daniel would faithfully point this pagan king to God Most High, speak truth when it could cost him his life, and even act with compassion when he had to prophesy coming judgment.

At the end of King Nebuchadnezzar's life, Belshazzar succeeded him as king of Babylon. Daniel, the respected and trusted adviser, must have moved largely into retirement. Maybe his advice seemed old fashioned and his wisdom too restrictive. The young king was wild and reckless, certainly irreverent, and during one wild party, he ordered the holy vessels from Jerusalem's temple to be used for his wine and revelry. But the party came to a screeching halt when a hand was seen writing on the wall inside the palace, its words unintelligible to all the partygoers. Terror struck the heart of Belshazzar, and the queen calmly reassured him that there was a good man who could surely help.

> There is a man in your kingdom who has the spirit of the holy gods in him. In the time of your father he was found to have insight and intelligence and wisdom like that of the gods. Your father, King Nebuchadnezzar, appointed him chief of the magicians, enchanters, astrologers and diviners. He did this because Daniel, whom the king called Belteshazzar, was found to have a keen mind and knowledge and understanding, and also the ability to interpret dreams, explain riddles and solve difficult problems (Daniel 5:11-12).

While Daniel served Nebuchadnezzar in humility and grew in wisdom and even warmth toward his foreign master, by the time Belshazzar took the throne, Daniel was no longer gentle in his rebukes. It seems time, age, and experience diminished his ability to deal with flat foolishness. It is easy to imagine that he didn't want to be summoned in the night to head to the palace for another one of the king's raucous parties. The young king offered gifts and the third highest position in the government to Daniel for an interpretation of the message. Daniel's response was curt—basically, "You can keep your stuff."

But he still interpreted the message. The Babylonian empire would fall into the hands of the Medes and Persians because of the pride of Belshazzar's heart. As Daniel put it, "You did not honor the God who holds in his hand your life and all your ways" (verse 23).

Daniel was immediately clothed in purple with a chain of gold fastened around his neck, and he was appointed the third ruler of the kingdom, possibly with his hair still a little tousled from being rudely awakened. To say that Daniel killed the buzz would be putting it mildly. This had turned out to be an unforgettable party.

It must have been mere moments later that they received the news of an approaching enemy army. That very night—with Daniel robed in purple, the young King Belshazzar sobering up, and the handwriting quite literally on the wall—the kingdom was invaded. Belshazzar was killed, and 62-year-old Darius the Mede received the kingdom.

I wonder if Daniel's and Darius's eyes met that night, if someone pointed out the distinguished older man standing awkwardly in a room full of drunks on the night of the fall of Babylon. Regardless, as King Darius appointed his new advisers and administration, Daniel again rose to the top.

What was it about Daniel that made him such a trusted man that kings of different ages and backgrounds would choose to make him their closest adviser? Was it his political prowess, his unparalleled intellect? Undoubtedly. But Scripture makes it clear that what distinguished Daniel was his excellent spirit: "Now Daniel so distinguished himself among the administrators and the satraps by his exceptional qualities that the king planned to set him over the whole kingdom" (Daniel 6:3).

Daniel's spirit shone like a beacon. In the middle of upheaval, opulence, indulgence, fear, and inevitable backbiting and scrambling for security, the light in the room was Daniel's character.

Though Daniel was likely in his early eighties at the time, he was considered to be indispensable because of his wisdom, and King Darius knew he would suffer no loss at the hands of Daniel. As we just saw,

"The king planned to set him over the whole kingdom" (verse 3). This decision did not please the political elite, and the other leaders of the nation scrambled to find charges against him—anything to keep Daniel from assuming this position of leadership. "The administrators and the satraps tried to find grounds for charges against Daniel in his conduct of government affairs, but they were unable to do so" (verse 4). They could find no complaint, no fault, no error, no corruption, no negligence. Daniel was faithful and trustworthy.

His impeccable character left his political opponents with little opportunity. "Finally these men said, 'We will never find any basis for charges against this man Daniel unless it has something to do with the law of his God'" (verse 5). In that meeting of dull bulbs, they agreed that they could trap Daniel, but only regarding his faithfulness to his God. When push came to shove, Daniel would choose his God over any role, any power, any reward—come what may.

May it be so in us. May it be so in our children. At the beginning of their lives, when their eyes are bright and the possibilities are endless, may they choose to obey their God and risk the scorn, judgment, and misunderstanding of others. May they walk in such a way that their faithfulness, loyalty, strong work ethic, and willingness to be used by God is what distinguishes them in their careers, communities, and homes. And when they reach their golden years, may it be said of them, "There is no one wiser. Over the course of their service, in the matters of their personal and professional life, we can find no fault."

Yes, it is possible for a person to live and serve in the midst of a corrupt generation with their character and faith intact. We have found such an example in Daniel, and we will find this same strength of character among other faithful servants of the Lord. Make no mistake, friend, the mess we are in has everything to do with our character when no one but God is watching.

Change can happen in our culture. It can happen in our home and in our children. But it starts with us.

Father,

My heart cry is to a raise a child who walks with You in integrity. Yet it seems that our culture's character is crumbling before my eyes. Arrest my heart with a vision for righteousness and change that begins in my home, envelops my child, and transforms our community. Start in me, Jesus. Start in me. Amen.

2

Brick by Brick

What Is Character?

> There is but one good; that is God.
> Everything else is good when it looks to
> Him and bad when it turns from Him.
>
> C.S. LEWIS

When Brendan, our oldest, told us that he wanted to get a real job last summer, Mike and I were thrilled. We were both raised in families that embraced hard work, and one of our core values is a strong work ethic.

Brendan got a job with our friend Sam. Sam is a builder by trade, an incredibly hard worker, and a retired army lieutenant colonel with three deployments in combat zones under his belt. By all accounts, he is an intense boss who's not afraid to raise up hard workers.

Brendan respects and admires Sam, so he was grateful for the job. If he'd known what was coming, he may not have been so eager. Sam and his wife, Jen, had purchased and reassembled an old barn on a portion of their property and planned to use it as a beautiful wedding venue in our stretch of rural West Michigan. To see the result now would leave you breathless.

At the beginning of summer, however, it was just a beautiful old barn with a pile of bricks in the basement. Sam and Jen had known from the beginning what they wanted the barn to look like. They scouted the area for brick aged with beauty to line the inside walls of the barn columns. Brendan's job was to help in all aspects of the barn remodeling project, but most of the summer he chiseled old mortar off the reclaimed bricks. The work was tedious, hitting bricks with a hammer day in and day out. By the time I would pick him up in the late afternoon, Brendan was covered in mortar dust, his hands blistered despite his leather work gloves and his fingers stiff from holding the hammer. He didn't really complain, but he would ask for back rubs, new gloves, and something a little more exciting to pack in his lunch box.

As I dropped him off at the barn one morning, Brendan invited me in to see his work. He unlatched the big door and slid it open. Dust hung in the air, and before us sat two pallets of bricks—clean bricks on one side and unclean bricks on the other. I asked him to show me how to do the job, and he pulled a brick onto the table, laid it square against another board, and chiseled the brick in front of me. As I gazed at the pile of bricks still to be cleaned, I groaned inwardly. Outwardly, I kissed my handsome teenager on the cheek, told him I was proud of him, and walked back to my minivan.

As I opened the car door to head home, I knew I could not do what that boy was doing. I could not sit and pound on bricks hour after hour, day after day, week after week.

The job didn't get easier with time. As the summer got hotter, cross-country practice began. Brendan would run four to five miles with his team and then go to an eight-hour job that involved hammering bricks, laying flooring, or cutting wood. Day by day, I knew that he was chiseling out a character quality that surpassed that of his mother. I wanted to see him develop grit and self-discipline, and he exceeded my expectations.

If you were to ask Brendan if he wants to do the same work next summer, he would probably tell you no, but he would quickly explain that the experience was good for him. The inner wrestling and mental fortitude it took to stay in one place and work shaped his character.

The same is true for us, friend. We are called to work day in and day out, laying the foundation upon which our children build their lives. We labor past the initial fun of the task and get to the point when we think we may fall apart instead of stay the course. This is where our own character is built, and it is also the anvil on which God begins to forge the character of our children.

"Mom, What *Is* Character?"

How can we live out something we cannot define? When it comes to the word *character* and the way it is used in society today, it is important to understand not only the word's origin, but the genesis of the concept. Over the last year I have ripped articles out of magazines, scoured bookstores, and pinned quotes on a corkboard on my quest to define character. I've purchased dozens of books that address the topic, but not one of them has succinctly defined it. Many of them list the same traits (honesty, empathy, courage), but none of them have explained why—across generations, demographics, and geography— the world has come to a consensus on that handful of virtues.

My senior-year Honors English teacher would spend the first five or ten minutes of each class expounding definitions of words that he thought we would need to know. I ate it up. My teacher's fascination with words has spurred my own. So, with a nod of recognition to Mr. Underwood, let me spell out for you my own definition of character.

Character is not your reputation. It is not who people think you are—whether classy and desirable or negative and off putting. It is not your accomplishments or a list of your natural talents. Character is who you really are, not the image you put forward on your best day.

Character is the inner governance and moral fiber of a person, evidenced in their speech, choices, actions, and attitude. It is the substance of who you are in the core of your being. It determines your priorities, bears weight in your decision making, and decides the relationships you keep and cultivate. Character is your moral nature that is revealed when no one applauds or is even around to notice, and it is built on the values you hold most dear.

If we were to ask any member of the general population if they agree with that definition, I feel confident the answer would be yes. However, the priority one places on being a person of upstanding character differs greatly. While people may give a nod to the moral high ground, society lives by an entirely different value system. All indicators seem to suggest that society believes poor character can be overcome by an individual's contributions to society, along with a winning personality, profitability, uniqueness, skill, and aptitude. The repercussions of this choice to devalue character can be seen and felt across our culture.

The Origin of Character

Where do we begin the discussion about character with our kids? We want them to live God-honoring lives, but we never want them to believe that their salvation depends on their behavior. We want our kids to know that they don't have to be good enough, but rather that in Christ there is grace enough. We want our children to experience the favor that comes from being a person who can be trusted and esteemed, but we don't want them to misunderstand for a minute, thinking that their worth or worthiness is found in these things. We want them to realize that they are not left to contrive a sense of morality on their own, nor are they left to meet society's sliding scale. Godly character is found in the nature, person, and Word of God, and it starts right in the first verse: "In the beginning God…" (Genesis 1:1).

What we are looking for is found in God. There was nothing that came before Him. He is the definition of everything honorable that we admire. "Through him all things were made; without him nothing was made that has been made" (John 1:3). All aspects of human integrity have God as their origin, and apart from Him integrity cannot be known or experienced. Those things we would call "good character" originate with God.

Though the world does not see God or know Him, it intuitively values His attributes. In its healthiest state, society values loyalty, goodness, generosity, and compassion. Though people are jaded and marred by sin, they still stop to notice self-sacrifice, love, and justice. They may struggle to find the words to articulate that they desire something trustworthy and good, but they will quickly identify disappointment and disillusionment in its absence.

Consider the following attributes of God as examples of the character a healthy society values.

God Is Light

We long for something that is consistent, trustworthy, and good. Even hardened criminals want somebody to have their back, cover them, and be loyal. Scripture tells us that "God is light; in him there is no darkness at all" (1 John 1:5). There is no corruption of character, no shadow side to be found in the heavenly Father.

Light is a symbol of righteousness, indicating a place where nothing can be hidden because all is visible. God is this place of trustworthiness. We may search in every corner of His vastness and find no hidden secrets. Yet His permeating light reveals our own darkness, hidden junk, and shadow sides. This knowledge is both comforting and terrifying, since sin lives and flourishes in darkness. We long for the time when there will be no need for the sun to light the day because God Himself will be our light, the One who has covered our sins and will banish darkness forever (Revelation 22:5).

God Is Good and Holy

Scripture clearly characterizes God as altogether good. Goodness is devoid of any evil actions, intentions, and inclinations. The Bible also refers to this as holiness, a complete absence of sin. The angels in God's presence cry out, "Holy, holy, holy is the LORD Almighty; the whole earth is full of his glory" (Isaiah 6:3).

We long for something unequivocally good. While we search for it in each other, we find this in God. The psalmist tells us to "give thanks to the LORD, for he is good; his love endures forever" (Psalm 118:29). Thanksgiving and praise are appropriate when we recognize that God's plan for us is good (Jeremiah 29:11), and He works all things together for our good as well (Romans 8:28). Though the world doesn't recognize the source of goodness, it certainly esteems its fruit—like trustworthiness, honor, and self-sacrifice.

God Is Gracious

Without knowing why, the world expects and hopes to be shown grace by others. When we're late for an appointment or miss a due date on a payment, we hope for a "grace period," a time when we will not face a consequence we have earned. We value those who show mercy and cover our flaws. This uncredited longing inside us is found in the nature and character of God: "The LORD is gracious and compassionate, slow to anger and rich in love. The LORD is good to all; he has compassion on all he has made" (Psalm 145:8-9). When we forgive those who have disappointed us or bestow favor on those who have not earned it, we are actively imaging God whether we know it or not.

God Is Just

Mankind is born with an undeveloped yet present sense of right and wrong. When this moral code is violated and our perceived rights are infringed upon, a cry for justice erupts out of us. This, too, flows from the character of God. "The LORD reigns forever; he has established his throne for judgment. He rules the world in righteousness and judges the peoples with equity" (Psalm 9:7-8). This hope for impartiality and desire for criminals to receive their due consequence is God's heart as well. Fortunately for Christ followers, God is able to satisfy the just part of His nature, which brings about His wrath, by laying the penalty for sin squarely on our Savior, Jesus. In fact, "the LORD longs to be gracious to you; therefore he will rise up to show you compassion. For the LORD is a God of justice. Blessed are all who wait for him!" (Isaiah 30:18).

God Is True and Faithful

The world would not know truth apart from God. In fact, one of Satan's first assaults on the world was the questioning of truth and God's word in Genesis 3:1-5. However, what Eve failed to realize in that cataclysmic moment was that God could not lie. It would violate His nature. "God is not human, that he should lie, not a human being, that he should change his mind. Does he speak and then not act? Does he promise and not fulfill?" (Numbers 23:19). It is no surprise, then, when His Son, Jesus, declares, "I am the way and the truth and the life" in John 14:6. Just as Eve's world crumbled when she believed a lie, so being deceived or outright lied to is an affront to humans today. Though all of us may not know why we put a premium on truth, we are hardwired to long for it.

Unfortunately, we are limited in our ability to keep our word. This is largely due to the changing of our minds or circumstances. But God is not limited in His ability to fulfill His Word. The prophet Isaiah writes, "LORD, you are my God; I will exalt you and praise your name, for in perfect faithfulness you have done wonderful things, things planned long ago" (25:1).

Even though God alone is completely true and trustworthy, we hope to find faithfulness in the people around us as well—someone who keeps their commitment even when it is difficult to do so. When marriages last, when someone perseveres in the face of great obstacles, the world notices. But God alone is perfect in His faithfulness toward us. Ultimately, this dependability causes us to lean in and trust. As Scripture says, "Those who know your name trust in you, for you, LORD, have never forsaken those who seek you" (Psalm 9:10).

God Is Love

"God is love" (1 John 4:8). When parents tenderly nurture a child, they image the love of God to the world. The satisfaction found in being deeply known and our idea of what constitutes love are found in the nature of God's love. Scripture goes as far as to define it for us in 1 Corinthians 13:4-8:

> Love is patient, love is kind. It does not envy, it does not boast, it is not proud. It does not dishonor others, it is not self-seeking, it is not easily angered, it keeps no record of wrongs. Love does not delight in evil but rejoices with the truth. It always protects, always trusts, always hopes, always perseveres. Love never fails.

This is the kind of love we long for, but it rarely surfaces in our reality. When it does, it is satisfying and deeply valued by most. The full extent of this love holds no earthly equivalent: "God demonstrates his own love for us in this: While we were still sinners, Christ died for us" (Romans 5:8).

God Is Patient

Wrapped up in God's love for us, we find His beautiful patience. He is willing to wait to discipline us and isn't rash in His words, reactions, or timing. Peter explains, "The Lord is not slow in keeping his promise, as some understand slowness. Instead he is patient with you, not wanting anyone to perish, but everyone to come to repentance" (2 Peter 3:9). God does not respond out of frustration, a sense of inconvenience, or anger.

God Is Compassionate

We long not just to be shown mercy, but for someone to step into suffering and brokenness beside us. The heavenly Father does this—it's who He is. The psalmist explains, "The Lord is gracious and righteous; our God is full of compassion" (Psalm 116:5). Isaiah also addressed this as he prophesied about the coming Messiah, Jesus: "Surely he took up our pain and bore our suffering…He was pierced for our transgressions, he was crushed for our iniquities; the punishment that brought us peace was on him, and by his wounds we are healed" (53:4-5). God does not stand at a distance from our pain and sickness, and in the ultimate act of compassion, He came to dwell among us.

It is awe inspiring to find that the attributes of character innately esteemed by humankind are found in God. Although fuzzy and undeveloped, society's general view of morality is shaped by the image of God that He has placed in each of us.

In the Beginning

From the first pages of the Word of God, we find that God created a world entirely good, a gleaming globe ripe with possibility, wonder, and light. The first man, Adam, was created in the image of God Himself, good and right (Genesis 1:27), and was tasked with bringing order and creativity to the world God had created. Adam was joined by a wife, also created in the image of God—beautiful, helpful, and good. Together they imaged God better than they could alone, and their union was honoring before the Lord. And on the seventh day, God rested from His work with a holy sigh to enjoy it all (Genesis 2:2-3).

This land of wonder and this relationship of mutual trust and holiness were soon broken. When Adam and Eve chose rebellion against God's command in Genesis 3, sin entered the world. What immediately followed was blame between the first couple, shame at their nakedness, and fear of the heavenly Father.

It's tempting to think the wheels fell off God's plan for bringing His image and glory to the earth, but all along His plan provided for this disfiguring of His image in the world. Revelation 13:8 tells us that the Lamb of God was "slain from the creation of the world." The Father planned from the beginning that He would send His Son to the world to rescue us because He knew that giving us free will meant we would stumble, fall, and choose our way over the path of righteousness.

The Image of God in Jesus

Though Scripture tells us that Jesus was with God at the creation of the world (John 1:1-2), infinite in power, Christ was then sent to the earth, stripped of the privilege and glory that was rightfully His, to fulfill a twofold rescue plan. The first aspect of that plan was to live a righteous life and die a substitutionary death in our place. Paul puts it this way:

> Christ Jesus…being in very nature God, did not consider equality with God something to be used to his own advantage; rather, he made himself nothing by taking the very nature of a servant, being made in human likeness. And being found in appearance as a man, he humbled himself by becoming obedient to death—even death on a cross! (Philippians 2:5-8).

Jesus, wonder of wonders, put on flesh and died to save us. Yet, in fulfilling that incredible purpose, He also fulfilled another purpose. The Savior lived a life on this sin-soaked planet and imaged God to the world. Colossians tells us that "the Son is the image of the invisible God" and that "God was pleased to have all his fullness dwell in him" (1:15,19). This means that to live with Jesus was to experience the character of God living in a broken world. Through Jesus, God repaired the pieces that the first image bearers had shattered and reestablished His standard for the world to see.

In every way, we can look to the Son and see the character that God requires. Our hearts long for that character to be realized in ourselves and our families. Asking, "What would Jesus do in my situation?" is an altogether appropriate question, because what we are actually asking is, "How would God, perfect in holiness and character, respond in my situation?"

The Image of Jesus in You

God's plan did not conclude with Jesus coming to bear His image. When Jesus defeated death, rose from the grave, and ascended back to the right hand of the Father, He sent His Spirit to dwell within us. Jesus explained to His disciples, "Very truly I tell you, it is for your good that I am going away. Unless I go away, the Advocate will not come to you; but if I go, I will send him to you" (John 16:7).

I love the phraseology of another translation, which says, "I tell you that I am going to do what is best for you. That is why I am going away. The Holy Spirit cannot come to help you until I leave" (CEV). Jesus was going to do what was best for us. While on earth, He lived in the parameters of a human body, occupying one space at a time. However, when Christ ascended to heaven, He sent His Spirit, limitless in scope and power, to dwell within those who would believe.

When Jesus rose from the dead, He not only defeated the condemnation the Fall brought into our lives, but He also defeated sin's right to grip us and keep us from righteousness. So we are brought into the plan of redemption God has had from the beginning. Through the power of the Holy Spirit working within us, God is in the process of "conform[ing] [us] to the image of his Son" (Romans 8:29). You see, friend, God's plan is for us to look like Jesus in our nature and character because Jesus looked like God. And by God's grace, we don't have to undergo this transformation alone.

In Pursuit of Goodness

It is a general grace of God to humankind that we can know, practice, and enjoy the character of God without knowing Him. Imagine if He had decided to withhold all joy, justice, peace, and righteousness from those who did not know Him. The world would have quickly descended into chaos. Because He is endlessly gracious, we can experience aspects of His divine character before we come to know Him. To that end, we can emulate and embody a godly character before coming into a relationship with Him.

I can think of dozens of really "good" people who love others, serve their community, and are extremely generous with their time and money. For example, my stepdad, Chuck, is one of the nicest guys I have ever known. He and my mom met at a divorce recovery workshop in a church in downtown Colorado Springs when I was growing up. He was a facilitator, and my mom, sister, and I were participants. What began was a friendship that would grow over the next three years.

Chuck became our friend and cheerleader as our little family did the work of recovering from a difficult divorce. When my mom and Chuck eventually became engaged, he offered me a job helping in the office of his custom home-building business. While running copies of blueprints and answering the phone, I was able to see firsthand how generous he was with difficult people. I watched and learned as he demonstrated patience with subcontractors who made mistakes and gracefully handled wealthy, sometimes demanding, homeowners, indiscriminate in his respect for both groups of people. In private, he was a generous stepdad—loving, supportive, and kind.

When I became a follower of Jesus in my late high-school years, he was encouraging and would often comment on the growth he had seen in my life. However, when it came to spiritual things, while he encouraged whatever made us grow and brought joy into our lives, he was disinterested in Christ. I often told others that if we were to get into heaven by good works and being good people, we would all line up behind Chuck. But that just isn't how the kingdom of God works.

The writer of Hebrews tells us that "without faith it is impossible to please God, because anyone who comes to him must believe that he exists and that he rewards those who earnestly seek him" (11:6). This means that although God values our character, what brings Him pleasure is not our behavior but rather our belief in what He did through Jesus.

As much as we value and esteem character and goodness, we are not measured by it in regard to salvation. Our problem is our sin, whether measured by a teaspoon or an ocean. When it comes to that weight around our necks, we are all doomed. "All have sinned and fall short of the glory of God" (Romans 3:23). The penalty for that sin, whether one act or a million, is death (Romans 6:23). What God is looking for is not our good works or even our good character, but faith alone.

Jesus said, "I am the way and the truth and the life. No one comes to the Father except through me" (John 14:6). And the apostle Peter explains, "Christ also suffered once for sins, the righteous for the unrighteous, to bring you to God. He was put to death in the body but made alive in the Spirit" (1 Peter 3:18). Christ alone won our freedom from sin and our reconciliation with the Father. This means that while we can live a "good" life apart from Him, it will be done through sheer willpower, without the help of the Holy Spirit, who is given to us when we are saved. And at the end of the day, all our effort will fall short regarding salvation. We are hopeless and helpless without Jesus.

After years of fervent prayers for his salvation, my stepdad—the man I still love and admire—gave his life to Christ. Now Chuck lives infused with the Holy Spirit. He is not a perfect man, but one whose character is being conformed into the image of Jesus. Hallelujah!

What Does This Mean for Us as Parents?

Now that we know that the character we admire and desire to cultivate in our families is found in the nature of God, how do we begin the process of yielding to the chiseling work of the Lord? Being shaped and conformed into the image of Jesus does not merely involve stripping away the bad, but also learning how to be molded by the trustworthy hand of God. We need to talk to our children about the plan for their character—but first, let's lay ourselves before the Lord and embrace the implications of being in the conforming process as well. This may change the aim of our parenting and discipling efforts and could help us release our kids from the burden of performing for our approval. The following are three focuses we can grab hold of today.

Find Him Faithful

We aren't alone in our efforts to form good character. God has not dropped us off on a corner and said, "Measure up, kid, and prove yourself to Me." Instead, He has paved the way for us to rest in Him and be transformed. God put on flesh and modeled in Jesus the life He asks us to live. Jesus imaged God for us, and then, upon our salvation by grace through faith, He sends His Spirit to make the restoration of God's image in us possible.

Jesus said, "The Helper, the Holy Spirit, whom the Father will send in my name, he will teach you all things and bring to your remembrance all that I have said to you" (John 14:26 esv). We are not abandoned to measure up by our own power, and neither are our kids. Yes, character is an inner governance, but for the Christian it is a governance by the Holy Spirit. Rather than being self-powered, we are enabled to walk in the Spirit; we are being conformed to the image of Jesus.

Find Him Lovely

We need to become students of God. Once we accept that our concept of true and good character comes from God and flows from Him, the only appropriate response is to draw near in worship. We must learn the ways of His character and study Him. We need to meditate on His goodness and seek Him in His Word.

There is no more worthy pursuit than the study of our glorious, good, loving God, and we need to train ourselves to esteem His godliness, those attributes that make Him who He is. We must love and value His holiness, goodness, gentle leading, perfect justice, and stead-fast love. We must admire, crave, and point to His beauty and wisdom. There is nothing more magnetic than a parent who is enthralled with his or her God. The most natural thing in the world is for children to admire and esteem the things their parents do, so imagine the limitless possibilities when a parent esteems God most.

Find Him Foundational

We must allow God to realign our expectations of our children and the nature of our instruction. We are not teaching our kids a behavior modification course for our pleasure or benefit. We are training our children to embrace the image of God and to be transformed into the image of Christ. The image of God is innate, hardwired in us as we begin life on this spinning globe, equal in measure between individuals. The forming of the image of Christ in us, however, is something that must be grappled with and acquired.

This means that we need to teach our children, even before they know Christ as Savior, that they should value what He values in others and ourselves. We need to focus on His designation of infinite worth. Then we can encourage them to be transformed by the renewing of their minds through His Word so that they will "be able to test and approve what God's will is—his good, pleasing and perfect will" (Romans 12:2). God's will at its most foundational level is the same for each child and for us, that we would lay down ourselves, cling to the cross, and begin to look like Jesus.

All of this may feel heady, but throughout the rest of this book we'll unpack this essential truth: There is a standard of character we are looking for, and it is found in the heavenly Father. The transformation we are longing for in our society, world, and homes is possible when we yield to God's Spirit. This carving of our character and that of our children is really all about living in the way of Jesus, being conformed to His image—thinking the way He thinks, serving those He would serve, and loving the way He loves.

Father,

I am amazed to see once again that all good things come from You. The character our world is aching for is found in who You are. Lord, I want to cooperate with the transforming work You are doing to forge the image of Jesus in me and my children. Open my eyes to see Your goodness all around me; help me begin to identify where I have departed from Your will and plan. I do believe that Your way is the best way for our society and my family. Change us, and start in me. In Jesus's name I pray, amen.

3

Welcome to the Revolution

Living Counterculturally

> We were settling for a Christianity that
> revolves around catering to ourselves
> when the central message of Christianity is
> actually about abandoning ourselves.
>
> DAVID PLATT

In the fall of 1857, Jeremiah Lanphier, an unassuming layman, invited people to a simple prayer meeting at the Old Dutch North Church on Fulton Street in New York City. Jeremiah had no training in theology or evangelism. He was simply a 49-year-old man who knew that his community needed prayer. The first meeting came, and halfway through the designated hour he was joined by one man. By the end of the hour they had six.

It was just a simple prayer meeting. "Lanphier had no way of knowing that it was the beginning of a great national revival which would sweep an estimated one million persons into the kingdom of God."[1] A couple weeks later, on October 14, the nation was hit by a crippling financial crisis. The prayer meeting soon drew crowds of more than 3,000 people, both white-collar and blue-collar workers.

Within six months, 10,000 businessmen gathered daily to pray in New York City. *Daily.* Revival fire not only changed the texture of this city at the crossroads of the world but also spread throughout the nation. What began in New York rolled to Philadelphia and beyond.

Perhaps the following commentary published in a Chicago newspaper sums it up best:

> So far as the effects of the present religious movement are concerned, they are apparent to all. They are to be seen in every walk of life, to be felt in every phase of society. The merchant, the farmer, the mechanic—all who have been within their influence—have been incited to better things; to a more orderly and honest way of life. All have been more or less influenced by this excitement.[2]

May it begin again in us. May our times with the Lord, fervently seeking Him, so shift culture that nothing and no one are left unaffected. May the world look at us and say, "I have no idea what's happening, but these people love us and Jesus."

Start a Revolution

A revolution is within our reach. The same Spirit that swept the nation in the late 1850s with prayer and new life in Christ is available to us today. Cultural change has happened in the past, and it can happen again. We can be reshaped and resurrected from a trend of decay. It begins with prayer, but we must also understand the dynamics of cultural change.

The very definition of counterculture involves a small group of people immersed in a larger culture with values, behavior, and rules of engagement differing greatly from their own. This subgroup of people lives in resistance to what they view as moral injustice, and they envision a life vastly different from that of the larger culture.

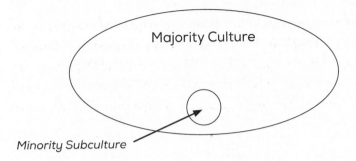

Majority Culture: "I Am My Own"

The key difference between majority culture and our Christ-following subculture is the approach to authority. The majority culture operates from the core view that people belong to themselves. They value independence, freethinking, and autonomy. We see this expressed in frustration and anger when the freedom to self-govern is threatened directly or indirectly. Adherents to the majority culture believe that the only wrong way to live one's life is the way that interrupts how someone else wants to live theirs, and they believe that restrictions on behavior and freedom are dangerous.

I find Jonathan Leeman's description of such suspicion of authority fascinating.

> The campaign that Western culture has been waging for several centuries *for* the individual has been a campaign waged *against* all forms of authority. From elementary school through graduate school, Western educators have taught us to question authority: the authority of the church because of what it did to Galileo; the authority of the king because of his usurpations; the authority of the majority because of its tyrannies; the authority of males because of their exercise of brute strength and acts of oppression; the authority of the Bible because of its alleged contradictions; the authority of science because of its paradigm shifts; the authority

of philosophy because of its language games; the authority of language because it has been deconstructed; the authority of parents because they're not cool; the authority of the market because of its extravagant inequalities; the authority of the police because of their fire hoses and night sticks; the authority of religious leaders because they'll make us drink the Kool-Aid; the authority of the media because of its biases; the authority of superpowers because of their imperialism. Are there any authorities left to question?[3]

The symptoms of this suspicion are everywhere, and it is leading to a huge undermining of our society's foundation of authority. Today's youth are also propelling the majority culture in unprecedented ways as they quickly adapt to and launch us into a new technological age.

Let us go no further without acknowledging that the church has all too readily adapted to the majority culture's skepticism. We, too, value self-governance, individualism, and freedom—things that are not innately negative. It's our search for these things outside the will of God that is the problem. Our responsibility is not to abandon this world and our society in a separatist way, heading for the hills or joining communes with fences. God is not calling Christ followers to form a militia, but rather to live under His authority and do some earthly good.

Christ-Following Subculture: "I Am Not My Own"

Raising a child of integrity is countercultural because Christ followers operate from an entirely different set of core values and beliefs than those of the majority culture. Let's look at some of these differences in detail and settle a vital issue from the beginning—namely, we are not our own; we belong to Christ.

Authority

While the majority culture stresses skepticism toward authority, we

Christ followers readily admit that there is an ultimate authority, and we are not it. We recognize that because God created us, we belong to Him and exist for Him and through Him. We live our lives under the authority of the revealed Word of God, the Bible, and we have a responsibility to obey the Lord.

Valuing All Life

Because God is the Creator of all, everything He creates is valuable. The pinnacle of His creative work was humankind. We are told that men and women were made in the image of God (Genesis 1:27)—and that image was imprinted upon every person regardless of their gender, age, race, size, shape, religion, and sin pattern. This means that Christians value the worth of every individual's life and determine that it should be protected and nurtured. This belief compels us not merely to advocate for the unborn but also to advocate for the ill, elderly, impoverished, and broken. It keeps us striving to see dignity and worth given to all people, not just believers, as we respect God's design and image within each person.

Integrity

Because we believers always live with an awareness of the pleasure and presence of the heavenly Father, we are to do the right thing even when it doesn't benefit us. We recognize that our actions in private must align with our public word. We maintain a wholehearted existence, seeing sin as something that hinders full, abundant life and costs more than we are willing to pay.

Putting Others First

We in the Christian counterculture believe that when Jesus said to "love your neighbor as yourself" (Matthew 19:19), He intended us to take that message seriously. This means that we live with others in mind, giving preference to the one behind us and cheering on the one in front of us. We look out for the good of not only our literal neighbors and those we feel comfortable around, but also the oppressed and the marginalized.

Work Ethic

Every little thing is relevant when we belong to the Lord, including the way we work. "Whatever you do, work at it with all your heart, as working for the Lord, not for human masters" (Colossians 3:23). This means that for us to live a life of integrity we must pursue excellence in the work of our hands—not with the goal of being approved of or promoted by men, but as an act of worship to God. We take pleasure in a job well done, unwilling to climb, crawl, and scratch to get to the top like those following the majority culture. Instead, we find contentment in the quality of our work, our diligence in completing a task, and our eye for the details others would pass over—all for the glory of the One we truly serve.

Speech

We as countercultural Christians are to be dignified in our speech, putting a premium on honesty and respect. Exodus 20:16 explains that people are not to bear false witness or lie about or to their neighbors—so as people of integrity, we carefully guard our mouths. Our speech bears the marks of purity, and we refuse to participate in profanity as image bearers of God. We speak about others with honor, doing "nothing out of selfish ambition or vain conceit," but rather "valu[ing] others above yourselves" (Philippians 2:3).

Forgiveness

Because we in this countercultural subgroup have been forgiven an eternal debt through Christ, we offer forgiveness to those who offend or hurt us. This is not a sign of weakness, but rather great inner strength. We entrust the matter of ultimate justice to the heavenly Father as the final judge, which means if we are not served justice in human courts, we will find it before the Lord. Jesus has taught us through His Word that we are to pray for our enemies, to be limitless in our forgiveness, and to play the part of the forgiver in any situation, thus fellowshipping with the Father (Matthew 5:44; 18:21-22).

Purity

We believers take the matter of purity seriously. We realize that purity is not just a mandate given by God regarding our sexuality, language, thoughts, and motives, but that it is a better way to live. We Christ followers understand that God's goal is not restrictiveness, but wholeness. The giving away of our hearts, minds, and bodies to things that violate God's laws—like sex outside the covenant of marriage, pornography, or even coarse humor—cheapens God's design for us, which is righteousness. Righteousness is purity of heart and mind that leads to right conduct and wholeness. We understand that the pursuit of these lesser things fractures hearts and homes, making an idol out of pleasure rather than living in true love and godliness. Therefore, we vow to set no vile thing before our eyes (Psalm 101:3) because it can lead us away from righteousness and the abundant life God longs to give.

Sexuality

In this counterculture we are to be courageous men and women, believing that God does not blush over our sexuality, but rather that He created sex for procreation and pleasure. We see sex as an important aspect of a marital relationship and celebrate it being reserved for that important relationship. When it comes to matters of gender, we agree with God's sovereign choosing for our lives, embracing the things that make us uniquely male or female.

Wisdom

We countercultural people value wisdom and good judgment. We seek after wisdom as treasure and work to align our lives with it. This wisdom reshapes our influences, helping us turn a listening ear to the Word and those who speak truth with dignity.

Success

At the end of our days, we believe success will be determined by the way we walked with the Lord, served Him in our generation, worked to win souls to Christ, and loved others. We live for the day when we'll hear the Lord say, "Well done, good and faithful servant!" (Matthew 25:23).

John Geddie and a Changing Tide

Could the majority culture truly change as one person sets their heart to image Christ and pull in a different direction? Undoubtedly. Consider the life and influence of a missionary named John Geddie.

John Geddie was born in Scotland in 1815 and immigrated with his family to Nova Scotia the following year. Although he was born into a Christian home, John was not an easy convert. Growing up, he had a fascination with foreign missions and heathen lands, and he even studied theology—but much to his parents' dismay, I'm sure, John did not personally put his faith in Christ until he was 19.

The Lord soon began to unfold His own path for young John. He was 22 years old when he became a Presbyterian pastor of a church on Prince Edward Island, and the following year he married his wife, Charlotte.

During his years as a minister, his passion for foreign missions took flight. At the time, there was little precedence for such colonial churches in the New World to send supported missionaries overseas, especially to work among unreached people groups. Completely convinced that this was the call on his life, he fought an uphill battle of conveying the need for foreign mission work. In a message he explained,

> To undertake a mission to the heathen is our solemn duty and our high privilege. The glory of God, the command of Christ and the reproaches of those who have gone to perdition unwarned, call us to it. With 600,000,000 of

immortal souls as my clients, I beg you to arouse yourselves
and to take a worthy part in this noble enterprise which
seems destined, in the arrangement of God, to be instrumental in achieving the redemption of the world.[4]

On November 30, 1846, under the direction and support of his
home church, John and Charlotte Geddie, together with their young
family, sailed for Polynesia as the first missionaries of a newly founded
South Seas mission. John knew the job before him would be dark: "In
accord with the Redeemer's command and assured of His presence,
we are going forth to those lands where Satan has established his dark
domain. I know that suffering awaits me. But to bear the Redeemer's
yoke is an honor to one who has felt the Redeemer's love."[5] In 1848
the family landed and settled on the small island of Aneityum, among
a native people steeped in the evils of cannibalism, idolatry and spirit
worship, and murder.

The Geddie family's first concern was their reception among the
natives, quickly followed by learning a new language that had no prior
written system. John needed to develop a deep understanding of the
culture to find language that would adequately convey the concept of
sin, the need for a Savior, and the abundant life found in Christ. But
he was up for the task.

He lived long years among the people of this island and others,
creating schools and assimilating with a purpose. The area was full of
wickedness and the abuse of women and the weak. According to one
historian, "The people were steeped in moral degradation. Licentious-
ness was rife, revenge was considered a sacred duty, forgiveness was a
word not to be found in the language and the spectacle of a happy heathen family, bound together by ties of love, was unknown."[6] The darkness was never far away, and the tradition of strangling a man's wife
upon his death was openly embraced.

Anywhere darkness has a foothold is a dangerous place to be, and
this labor was not without cost to John. As he traveled, he was often

threatened and sometimes injured with clubs, stones, and spears. I imagine it was a very lonely and discouraging time.

Then the tide changed.

> One day Geddie came upon a group of women wailing piteously and rubbing a man's corpse with broken leaves. Some were pulling their hair and shrieking violently. The man's widow, an attractive young girl, sat nearby expecting to be strangled. Geddie said, "This woman must not be killed," and started leading her from the scene. Immediately some men assaulted him, knocked him to the ground and seized the young widow. While some of the women held down the girl's arms and legs the men proceeded to strangle her. When Geddie again tried to intervene, men with clubs drove him away. The murderous deed was by this time completed.[7]

John refused to back down and confronted the men with the truth of the gospel. They had just completed an act that was heinous in the eyes of God. Struck by his words, conviction fell on these men.

In time there was a change of heart among the people. John not only taught new believers of salvation but also noted that it was their responsibility to reach their own people for Christ. The gospel began to spread and saturate the lives of the natives. Light began to pierce the darkness. As if a dam had cracked, salvation swept the island and natives came to Christ, leaving behind the revenge culture and cannibalism that had gripped them. Schools and churches were filled with people seeking a new way, native missionaries were sent to evangelize other islands, and the moral tide turned.

This account begs some questions: Is it possible for such a dramatic shift to occur in today's majority culture so that our nation's faith and moral tide could turn as well? Could such a change happen today? Could revival fire sweep across our lost, dark, and aching world?

What we are looking for is a tipping point. A point when the pull of the minority counterculture reaches a moment of fullness, and society begins to change. About countercultural movements, one writer expresses, "When oppositional forces reach critical mass, countercultures can trigger dramatic cultural changes."[8]

Could our "oppositional forces" be the light of the gospel and our children of character? Could our kids be the small minority culture of light whose oppositional working is evidenced by their hope in Jesus, drive for the gospel, untainted character, and love for their neighbor?

Such change has happened before, and by God's grace and with faith, it can happen again. The awakening to this mission happens one child at a time. However, at one unforeseen and dramatic moment—with the Holy Spirit's help—critical mass can be reached, and the tide can be shifted.

Reaching Critical Mass

I've turned the phrase over and over in my mind: "When oppositional forces reach critical mass, countercultures can trigger dramatic cultural changes."[9]

What is critical mass? It is "the minimum amount of something required to start or maintain any project or venture."[10] Historically, believers call the moment of momentum shift "revival."

This desire to see sweeping change and revival in our nation burns within me. What will it take to reach critical mass in our lifetime? This question drives me and has changed the trajectory of my life. I spent the summer of 2014 studying biblical and historical revival, looking for any commonality between them. What grew inside me as a result of that time of study was an unshakable desire to see God do it again, to bring a tectonic shift toward Christ in our generation and the next.

I believe revival can happen in our lifetime. Not the kind that slays people in the Spirit under white tents with strings of lights on hot summer nights, but the kind that defines a generation. The kind that so radically shapes the world that it must be discussed in history books as another Great Awakening. The common point between historical and biblical revivals is this: Prayer always precedes revival. It begins with a handful of people who lay themselves before the Lord in humility and ask for Him to move among them again.

Friend, are you a revivalist? Do you desire to see God work in such a fresh movement of the Spirit that our families, children, and nation are changed? Do you want to see revival accomplished not just so that we will experience a return to morality but so that people will walk in the full and abundant life found in Christ? I do.

The burden that God gave me for our children and their schools was very specific. I pray for many things—the leaders of our nation, awakening in the church, the poverty in my community. But for now the commission on my heart is to proclaim Christ to the next generation.

As I've reflected on what it would take to reach the tipping point in our culture, I've discerned three steps we must take as parents today.

1. We must plead with God for revival through prayer.

For every historical and biblical revival, prayer was an integral part of the process. God does not ignore our desperate prayers for Him to work and move on behalf of a generation. Gratefully, He is a magnet to those who need Him.

Now is the time when we must get on our knees for the lives of our children. The prophet Jeremiah charged his generation to awaken to the needs of their children and plead with the Lord for deliverance and movement. He pled, "Arise, cry out in the night, at the beginning of the night watches! Pour out your heart like water before the presence of the Lord! Lift your hands to him for the lives of your children, who faint for hunger at the head of every street" (Lamentations 2:19 ESV). Surely we must heed the same call; our children need our desperate prayers on their behalf.

2. We must immediately begin teaching our children about God, righteousness, and the authority of Scripture.

No matter where our kids are on their journey of faith, we parents must continue talking about the Lord and His righteous standard for our lives. Regardless of their reception of this truth, we need to press our effort in teaching them to live righteously, speaking of Christ often. There is no time for delay, and there will be no better time to do the molding and shaping necessary to prepare their hearts to receive Christ and follow Him. One season leads to the next, and the next will rarely be better or less busy for doing the hard work of training our kids.

Imagine if the mothers of people like John Geddie, John and Charles Wesley, Charles Spurgeon, Saint Augustine, or George Müller—all of whom were prodigals or relatively late acceptors of the gospel—had waited till their children were eager to learn about Jesus to begin teaching them about God, His Word, and His ways. Many of our founding mothers and fathers in the faith did not walk with Christ until adulthood, far past the times when their own mothers had hoped. However, their parents did the hard work of planting the seeds of faith while the ground of their children's hearts seemed hard. Those parents taught them the Word, raised them to choose righteousness, and prayed for years for them to walk with the Lord. Though many of these children did not make an early decision to follow Jesus, their mothers' training still bore fruit when they ultimately chose Christ.

This is why we must begin today. It is never too early to start training our children to love and obey God.

3. We must do the work inside us to cultivate personal revival.

The answer to our character crisis is Jesus. The change we want to see is found in Him, and we cannot expect this change to begin with others. It must begin with us.

Revival is a satisfied longing for God's presence and power in our lives as demonstrated by a fresh movement of the Holy Spirit. The very notion of "revival" assumes that at one point in your spiritual walk you were alive, fresh, and growing. You can't "revive" something that was never alive in the first place.

Friend, are you experiencing growth and an awareness of God's presence and power in your life right now? This doesn't mean every moment of your life feels like holy fire; it may mean you are in a faith slugfest, clinging to the Lord in disappointment and disillusionment but choosing again and again to press in and go deeper still.

We cannot lead our children into a deeper relationship with God than the one we ourselves have experienced and known. If we are longing for a moral turn in them and in our society, we must go first, laying aside every sin that entangles us and running after Him (Hebrews 12:1).

I have known years of growth and sunshine with the Lord in which every day seemed better than the last. And I have known seasons and even years of a heaviness and depression that would not lift despite my prayers. In such dry and difficult seasons, it is most important to seek God with our whole hearts, believing His promise that, despite our feelings, He draws near to those who seek Him (James 4:8). May we say with the psalmist, "We will not turn away from you; revive us, and we will call on your name. Restore us, LORD God Almighty; make your face shine on us, that we may be saved" (Psalm 80:18-19).

Friend, let's lean in and believe that we could be the parents whose sustained prayers bring about a sweeping revival. Oh may it be so, Lord.

Heavenly Father,

What would it take to reach a moment of critical mass in our nation? Show me, and I will pursue it. Would You ignite a desire for revival that begins in me, spreads to my family, and infects the world? Ready the soil of our hearts for a harvest of righteousness. Jesus, You are the answer to the problems we face. Grow in me a heart for lost people and remove any calluses that have grown and caused me to see any need as greater than the need for revival. In Jesus's name, amen.

4

Get Your Toes Back Where They Belong

Time for an Honest Assessment

> The community of the saints is not an "ideal" community consisting of perfect and sinless men and women, where there is no need of further repentance. No, it is a community which proves that it is worthy of the gospel of forgiveness by constantly and sincerely proclaiming God's forgiveness.
>
> DIETRICH BONHOEFFER

It was a beautiful day. I had turned my chair so I could watch three-year-old Brendan play with his cousins on the driveway. Before this, I had taken him by the hand and shown him his boundaries. He could play in every direction except one—the way that led to the road. There was a crack in the driveway delineating where he needed to stop to be safe. In every direction but one there was freedom, opportunity, and potential for joy.

But you intuitively know what happened, don't you? Maybe because you are a parent or because you know deep down that you would have been tempted to take the same next steps my son took.

He played for half a minute within bounds and then made a beeline directly over to the line on the ground. With a hand up, I signaled to my friend to wait a minute, and we both gave Brendan our full, silent attention to watch what would unfold.

He walked directly to the line and paced along it. He shuffled his feet back and forth. Then slowly, ever so slowly, he put his chubby little toes over the line. That's when he looked back at me with a mixed expression, equal parts exhilaration, curiosity, fear, and sass.

"Now *that* is putting one big, hairy toe over the line," my friend whispered to me.

It was.

It is time we own our rebellion. God has set boundaries for living just like the boundary I made for Brendan on the driveway. In turn, we march right to the lines God has drawn and put our toes across them.

Countercultural parenting involves accepting and operating from the understanding that we are born with a sin nature. Some people call it "inherited sin," tracing back to Adam and Eve, and others call it "original sin" because Adam's sin produced a morally corrupt nature in all of us, and in turn sin is counted against all of us.[1] Furthermore, we all willingly and actively sin against the Lord and one another. Romans 3:23 is clear on this point: "All have sinned and fall short of the glory of God." First John 1:8 tells us that "if we claim to be without sin, we deceive ourselves and the truth is not in us," and later, "If we claim we have not sinned, we make [God] out to be a liar and his word is not in us" (verse 10).

This means that countercultural parents are not shocked by the sin nature in themselves or those around them, and they are certainly not surprised to find that their own kids are sinners as well. After all, each of us was born into this condition, and each of us, apart from the redemption found in Jesus, lives a life marked by it.

As countercultural parents, we steadfastly refuse to be judgmental about another's sin while missing our own. Rather, we guide our family in the path of repentance and forgiveness, and we walk in the freedom found on the other side. First, however, we must do the work of putting aside "the sin that so easily entangles" (Hebrews 12:1).

Consider the Data

Be sure you know the condition of your flocks,
give careful attention to your herds.
PROVERBS 27:23

It is extraordinarily difficult for me to stand back and assess a situation that involves my own failure. Can I analyze problems in our government? Sure. Want me to identify the crazy in my kid's schools? You bet. Can I show you the nonsense within the walls of my church? Absolutely. But within my own home, it is incredibly difficult to shove aside feelings of failure and take an inventory of what is happening in the lives, behavior, and needs of my family.

To own that my child has a problem with anger, honesty, or her work ethic means facing the shame, guilt, and feelings of inadequacy as a parent. It is far easier to bury my head in the sand, run to the next activity, or skirt the issue. But if we as parents own the problem in our kids, calculate its depth, try to understand its genesis, and do the hard work of uprooting it—teaching or reteaching, and training in new behavior patterns—we will gain incalculable understanding in order to move forward.

Why would we resist the process of evaluation within our homes? Perhaps it is because the behavior of our children causes us embarrassment or shame. Maybe it's guilt that keeps us from prayerfully sifting through our patterns and processes to identify places that need our attention. At worst, it might be the inability to see the plank in our own eye (or family situation), preferring to pick at the specks in others' eyes (Matthew 7:3-5).

Author Jon Acuff gives a neutral name to our self-assessment findings. He calls our analysis "data." I love the term *data* when describing our kids' behavior because data doesn't have feelings; instead, data is generally just something on a spreadsheet to be learned from and considered. Calling our analysis of our children's lives "data" removes the anger, frustration, pride, and defeated mindset that often goes along with sensitive areas. It allows us to tackle the problems unemotionally and, hopefully, more practically. Acuff explains, "When you ignore data, you embrace denial…Denial is neon in others and invisible in you…Data doesn't lie, though. It is not swayed by emotion. It is not subject to the drunken whims of feelings. Disaster is always the final destination of denial."[2] When it comes to the character issues my children face, disaster just isn't an option.

Trouble, hardship, and grief are the final destination of parents who fail to take a frequent inventory of their children's character situations. Although we can experience pain when we face trouble in our marriages, our children, or the places in which we are dropping the ball, we can begin to heal and rebuild when we separate our emotions from the situation and objectively assess the scope of the problem. We're just gathering data. We cannot confront something we will not drag to the front of our consciousness. We cannot repair what we will not assess, and we cannot fortify what we will not own.

Character Assessment

I want to take you through an exercise assessing your child's current character choices. We will use the apostle Paul's charge to Timothy found in 1 Timothy 4:12 as our springboard: "Don't let anyone look down on you because you are young, but set an example for the believers in speech, in conduct, in love, in faith and in purity."

Before we begin, stop and pray that the Lord would highlight areas you need to see and concentrate on. This is not a character *assassination* of our kids; this is a character *assessment*. We need to be able to spot their strengths as well as their weaknesses, and there are always areas of strength. This cannot be a time when we merely condemn ourselves as parents or allow shame to take root. We can't allow anger to develop at our children, and we can't consider the current situation beyond salvage. Rather, we must discover the cracks, holes, and fault lines and begin again. Remember, "there is now no condemnation for those who are in Christ Jesus" (Romans 8:1). You can still be known by the courage it takes to make the repair and not the mess that existed in the beginning. Character begins when we steadfastly refuse to stay in the muck.

Assessments seem to work best when beginning with areas that are easy to identify and then systematically moving on from those places into the deepest areas of life. For the sake of clarity, this assessment uses phrasing associated with a daughter. However, the questions can apply to your son, your spouse, or even yourself. Change can only happen when you outline the problems facing you.

In Speech

Does my child's speech reflect the truth about the situation? Is she manipulative with her words, or does she allow others to make their own decisions? Does she complain and whine? Does she argue, interrupt, or blame others? Does she gossip, slander, nitpick, or degrade? Is she critical, profane, angry, aggressive, or defiant? Does she refuse to speak up when truth or righteousness need a voice? Do my child's words point to a life of self-righteousness or hypocrisy?

In Conduct

Does the way my daughter conducts herself demonstrate value for the life of others? Does she behave recklessly, aggressively, or abusively? Does she maintain healthy limits, or does she overindulge? Is my girl wise and given to understanding, or is she prone to embrace and celebrate folly? Is she a good steward of her resources and the earth? Is she resilient in the face of adversity? Will my daughter obey the laws of the land, or will she consider herself the exception? Does she value hard work, self-discipline, and follow-through?

In Love

Does my daughter extend herself to meet the needs of others? Does she act in the best interest of others even when it is inconvenient? Is she quick to abandon others emotionally or relationally? Does she keep a record of wrongdoing, or is she patient with the faults of others? Is my daughter demanding or self-seeking? Is she self-sacrificing in her behavior? Does she show partiality or devalue the lives of those who are unattractive to her?

In Faith

Does my daughter practice an unswerving commitment to faith? Does she actively demonstrate belief in the deity and lordship of Christ? Does she practice spiritual disciplines out of duty or out of a heart of love? Does my girl value and view the Bible as the infallible Word of God? Is her faith resilient when tested and tried? Has she laid aside things that distract her from the worship of the Father?

In Purity

Does my daughter make choices to behave and dress modestly? Does she watch shows that promote sexually promiscuous or explicit behavior? Are the intentions of her heart sexual purity and the protection of others in this area? Does she often place herself in situations where she will face temptation? Is she lustful, behaving provocatively outside the confines of marriage? Does she listen to or read about inappropriate sexual behavior? Does she cling to areas where she has previously caved to sexual sin? Does she affirm the biblical standard of marriage—in the context of heterosexual relationships—as the only place for sexual relations?

Surveying the Ruins

If you are anything like me, then your heart has been filleted and laid bare by these questions. If I am honest and assess myself—my heart and home—in addition to our daughters and sons, I am nearly undone. In every area of the above assessment, I see places of sin and brokenness in my life and the lives of my children. If there is one area of strength, it is met with equal measures of ruin in another area.

Rest assured, we are not alone in surveying the moral bankruptcy within our culture and ourselves. What will make us countercultural is our desire to take responsibility for our sin, confess it, and begin again.

Repentance Is RARE

If we claim to be without sin, we deceive
ourselves and the truth is not in us.
1 JOHN 1:8

There is no room for self-righteousness in the life of a Christ follower. Simply bearing the name Christian admits that we needed rescuing. To fail to address and admit our sin and responsibility in the character chaos that surrounds us does not add to our righteousness. To the contrary, those whom God esteems are the humble in heart who see exactly how flawed they are, how culpable they are in the trends of their community toward unrighteousness in word and deed.

Fortunately for us, Scripture is full of men and women who found themselves in the presence of the Lord and laid themselves bare before Him. The result is certainly not what we would expect at the revelation of the darkness that lies within. The godly repentance of one such man, the prophet Isaiah, brought about a personal revival and set him on a mission that changed the trajectory of not only his life, but the nation of Israel as well.

Recognize the Almighty

Agree with God

Repent

Engage in new behavior

R—Recognize the Almighty

The prophet Isaiah's personal revival began with an encounter with the Lord Almighty in a vision. During a time of personal grief over the demise of a great king, and in the shadow of judgment facing the nation of Israel, God gave Isaiah a fresh awareness of the unparalleled holiness of God. Isaiah 6 describes the scene in four powerful verses (verses 1-4) that include an exalted throne, smoke and glory filling the room, and breathtaking thundering as the angels cried out, "Holy, holy, holy is the LORD Almighty; the whole earth is full of his glory" (verse 3).

When it comes to repenting and leading our kids to do the same, we must first acknowledge who God is. Because character is defined by God's nature, we must recognize the part of His character that has been dishonored by our actions. God is in the process of transforming us into the image of Jesus (Romans 8:29), so our sin is falling short of imaging God to the world.

When our children lie, they misrepresent our God, who is truth.

When they give way to anger, they distort the image of God, who is patient.

If they slander, steal, or use the name of the Lord in vain, they participate with evil when God is holy.

If they behave selfishly, they have lost sight of the Servant-King.

When we spend time considering the greatness of our God, freshly encountering His holiness, a deep sense of humility grows in us.

A—Agree with God

In response to being in the presence of God Almighty, Isaiah cried out, "Woe to me!…I am ruined! For I am a man of unclean lips, and I live among a people of unclean lips, and my eyes have seen the King, the LORD Almighty" (Isaiah 6:5).

Notice the two-part confession of sin. Isaiah confessed that he, himself, was a man of unclean lips, and therein he admitted his personal shortcoming. He recognized that he was unworthy to stand before the holy Lord of hosts. After evaluating our own speech, conduct, love, faith, and purity, surely we can acknowledge the same. We are men and women of unclean lips.

In the second part of the confession, Isaiah owned the sin of his nation. He dwelled among a people of unclean, unworthy mouths, unfit for the presence of such holiness. These realities left him slack-jawed; neither he nor his people were fit to behold a God as flawless and good as the One he beheld.

Our culture does not want to acknowledge that there is a moral standard for our behavior. However, Christ followers know different. We must agree with God that He holds and defines that standard and that it is good and right. We need to help our kids understand God's standard and agree that the way He has called us to live is the right way. Until our children (and we ourselves) realize that the problem is not getting caught and experiencing consequences but rather breaking of God's standard, we are not done with our job of helping them understand the ramifications for their poor character choices.

After times of reflection, I must acknowledge that there are idols in my life that distract me from following Jesus wholeheartedly. I often find that the words I speak take life from others instead of giving life. Sometimes, like Isaiah, I'm even led right to my knees at the staggering realization that our nation's sins are piled to the sky. I have to agree with God that He is right in any judgments against our nation.

R—Repent

Isaiah's atonement for sin came from a flaming coal taken from the altar of God and pressed to his lips by an angel (Isaiah 6:6-7). The angel said, "See, this has touched your lips; your guilt is taken away and your sin atoned for" (verse 7). On this side of the cross of Christ, we need only confess our sins, ask forgiveness, and walk in repentance. "If we confess our sins, he is faithful and just and will forgive us our sins and purify us from all unrighteousness" (1 John 1:9).

The Greek word for repentance (*metanoia*) means more than just regret or sorrow. It means to turn around, to change direction and to change our minds about sin. In the New Testament, the word *repentance* is always used in reference to a changing of the mind, a choice to leave behind sin and a resolution to pursue righteousness.[3] John the Baptist told people to "produce fruit in keeping with repentance" (Luke 3:8). This means that we don't just say, "I'm sorry," while planning to sin again. And it certainly does not mean that we are just sad we got caught.

We need to be sure we are teaching our kids that actions are proof of a heart change and that fruit is expected. We need to be the first to spot our kids laying aside poor character and to notice the new fruit of positive character. When our children have confessed and repented, we as parents need to resolve that, like the heavenly Father, we will forgive and move on.

E—Engage in New Behavior

Our response after we repent is crucial. God asked who would go for Him, and Isaiah responded, "Here am I. Send me!" (Isaiah 6:8). Isaiah's repentance led to mission.

We, too, need to get busy putting on new behavior that will grow our character in the opposite direction of our sin. For me, this has involved tons of Scripture memorization involving the problem with which I'm struggling. I'm instilling this in my kids by trying to be sure they understand not only the behavior that God wants them to take off but also what He would call them to "put on." As the apostle Paul teaches,

> You were taught, with regard to your former way of life, to put off your old self, which is being corrupted by its deceitful desires; to be made new in the attitude of your minds; and to put on the new self, created to be like God in true righteousness and holiness (Ephesians 4:22-24).

There it is again—we were created to be like God, transformed into

His image to point people to Jesus. It isn't enough just to avoid sin; we have to get busy putting on righteousness, goodness, and faith. In our home, this involves making a plan for "next time." The next time we come up against this situation, how should we respond? What should we do differently or say instead? What would be the most honoring choice we could make? How can we "put on" the fruit of God's Spirit inside us—love, joy, peace, and so on?

Countercultural parenting involves good coaching, not just good discipline. This line of questioning and then the implementation of the findings is a setup for a character comeback, an opportunity to see character renewed or rebuilt. God does not expect perfection from us; in fact, He sent Jesus because we couldn't be perfect. But He does expect His children to begin again. This forging ahead with godliness in mind is the ground from which something new can grow, fertile ground for a fresh working of the Spirit and new character choices.

Steps to Prepare for Your Own Character Comeback

1. *Own your sin in the presence of God.* Sin-laden parents hand down heavy generational patterns to their children. Do your kids a favor; deal with your stuff.

2. *Lay it aside.* The writer of Hebrews tells us to get rid of anything that mars the image of Christ in us, tossing aside sin that prevents us from running after Jesus. He says, "Let us throw off everything that hinders and the sin that so easily entangles. And let us run with perseverance the race marked out for us, fixing our eyes on Jesus, the pioneer and perfecter of faith" (Hebrews 12:1-2).

3. *Steer clear.* Presuming that you can resist sin's charms and pitfalls is a recipe for disaster. Sin always takes us places we

do not want to go and ruins our lives when we get there. Flee!

4. *Find accountability.* The enemy is deeply involved in the temptations we face; don't fight these battles alone. "Better is open rebuke than hidden love. Wounds from a friend can be trusted" (Proverbs 27:5-6). Call in a trusted friend and ask for prayer and help in walking a new path.

5. *Stay in the Word.* God's Word is the best guide for helping us steer clear of sin traps and remain in steadfast character. It is alive, active, and relevant for the issues we face (see Hebrews 4:12-13). Ask the Lord to bring His words to mind as you face this battle.

Owning Our Blind Spots

My ministry requires enough travel that I have been forced to retire three suitcases that were worn through from airport abuse and over-packing last year. I deeply enjoy serving others through teaching, and as a result it is not unusual for me to miss meals, sleep, and home. While most people would crave a quiet room in which to recover after a long day at a conference, I long for quiet and a spot next to someone with whom I have a deep relationship.

Mike and I decided a couple of years ago that, in order to serve the Lord with longevity, whenever possible I would have a traveling companion. This was one of the wisest decisions we have made, and it keeps this introverted extrovert in a good place. However, a few times a year, taking a companion with me just isn't possible, and I've come to expect that in these times the Lord will reveal Himself to me in a brand-new way.

Last year I made a trip to Philadelphia that required me to travel alone. From start to finish it was a memorable journey. I began by making a pact with myself not to go to my hotel room and collapse into fast food and Netflix after a long day. Then I had an afternoon with the Lord that I will never forget. I lay down in bed that night and thanked Him for being so close, for delighting me and being my companion. I checked my flight times and made a mental note that I would love to sleep in if possible, but that if I woke up early enough, I would go downtown and look for the Liberty Bell.

Sure enough, my eyes popped open at 6:00 a.m., and I was wide awake. By 8:00 a.m. I was on the road headed to find the Liberty Bell. It was a quiet morning on the streets of Philadelphia, and I was able to park across the street from the exhibit—directly in front of a coffee shop that served up a mean cappuccino while I skimmed a guidebook. I set out with two and a half hours to spend exploring—certainly not enough time to be thorough, but I was ready to experience what I could.

In that time I read and walked through all the Liberty Bell exhibits, watched the videos, and had my picture taken. I then made my way across the street and saw Independence Hall, the building where the Declaration of Independence and the United States Constitution were written. I walked along the cobblestone streets and through the nearly empty Benjamin Franklin Museum on Chestnut Street, then decided I was close enough to see Betsy Ross's house and Delancey Street. It was an incredible morning learning and exploring, and I could see God's provision for me and our nation.

The night before I had seen two small boys run into the street to wash the windows of the cars stopped at an intersection. They were dressed in worn clothes and were looking for tips. I smiled at them and waved, but the light turned green before they made it to my car. The following morning, with a cappuccino in hand while walking the streets, I saw homeless people lying in the entryways of buildings. The most devastating sight for me was a young woman, obviously pregnant, propped up against a newspaper box with no shoes on her feet.

With each of these encounters, my insides turned, and I prayed. "Lord, what do you want me to see? What do you want me to learn and do?" As I walked, I wondered to myself if I was usually blind to the needs that surrounded me as I went about my day.

I slowed my walk at the corner of Market Street in front of the Liberty Bell exhibit to read the new signs that focused on the issue of slavery in the homes of America's Founding Fathers. Particularly piercing was the story of a slave girl in President George Washington's home who would listen outside the door as Martha Washington read the Bible to her granddaughters before bed.

My heart went to my throat. Our country may have been built on a Christian value system, but quite clearly, even the Founding Fathers had their blind spots. I wondered to myself how it could seem good and right to own people, use people to physically build a nation built upon the idea of freedom.

As I watch the news and consider the past, it is clear to me that every generation, every leader, every parent has the potential to miss something. A desire for peace can lead us to passiveness, condoning behavior we know is wrong or disrespect toward those who try to lead. This has been true in the issues of slavery, voting rights, gender discrimination, segregation, systemic poverty, and on and on. It is entirely possible to have a heart for the Lord and overlook an area of our lives where God wants to correct our thinking.

The thought that I may have a blind spot, a place where I am not correctly imaging God to the world and my children, is humbling. It isn't just my son with his eyes set toward the boundary line; I am the one who puts my toes over the line. I'm actively asking the Lord to search my heart and help me see the areas where I am not living in step with His Spirit. I want a chance to repent and to write a different legacy. *Father, open my eyes and show me.*

> *Father,*
>
> *I'm so grateful that You are slow to anger and abounding in love. Thank You for the forgiveness that is found through Jesus. I confess I'm in way over my head when it comes to cultivating*

character in the life of my child. I need You to help me recognize warning signs, to see things that I might miss, and to catch my child in praiseworthy moments. Keep watch over my own steps, Lord. I need You to guide us all on paths of righteousness for Your name's sake. In Jesus's name, amen.

5

Severe Discipleship

Totality: Obedience That Begins with Love

> Salvation is free, but discipleship
> costs everything.
> BILLY GRAHAM

When I first came to truly know and love the Lord, I was more than halfway through high school. Up until that point, I think I had heard the gospel a handful of times. I knew that Jesus had died to be our Savior, and I accepted that I needed Him. However, I had never heard—or at least never grasped—that this Jesus who died and rose for me wanted my entire life. I can't recall a single time when I heard that God expected not only to save my soul but to get the rest of me too. That I would belong to Him, He would be my leader, and, for the rest of my days, I would not belong to myself.

If I had grasped God's right to lordship over me early on, things would have turned out differently. I was the kid who prayed at Vacation Bible School at five years old, asking Jesus to save me, and again in middle school at a Young Life camp, but none of it made any sense until someone explained what I was missing: I was not my own. I had changed teams; I was a part of the light and could have no fellowship with darkness.

I envisioned my life as a grid of sorts, filled with different life compartments and activities. I had a box for my dad's family, and a box for my mom's. There was a boyfriend box, a sports box, a school box, and a grades box. Soon there were boxes for my entertainment, money management, plans for my future, and music choices. Inevitably, there was a box for sin, and another I labeled "new faith."

The problem arose one day when I realized that Jesus's plans weren't supposed to be kept in a box—one small, sacred corner of my life. It sure seemed that Jesus meant it when He told people to leave everything and follow Him. I realized that His messages touched every aspect of life, and I responded with both enthusiasm and reservation. I was eager to embrace the truth that Jesus wanted to heal all the areas of my life, but I was appalled at the idea that He might want to weigh in on who I wanted to date or my arguments with my sister.

The message of lordship—that God wants all of a person's life—is at the core of being a disciple, a countercultural man or woman of character. The concept of lordship flies in the face of every message the world teaches. For our children, this means they will be called a "goody-goody"—or worse, they will be considered radical and dangerous. Regardless of the world's response, though, the call remains: "Leave it all and follow Me."

Radical Love and Obedience

I don't always want to admit that God calls us to a severe discipleship. That He wants us to count the cost of following Him and find Him worthy of leaving our plans, preferences, security, and perhaps even safety behind. It certainly isn't my leading statement in most conversations about faith, but it is the bottom line when it comes to following Christ.

It is easier to represent the God who loves us no matter what than the One who wants our devotion with *all* our heart, *all* our soul, and *all* our strength (Deuteronomy 6:5). The message that God wants the entirety of our being feels extreme, especially when our deepest desire is to be in charge of ourselves. We don't want people to boss us. We want to be self-governed, self-appointed, and self-sufficient.

There was a time when my daughter stood and looked at me with her little hands on her hips and said, "Don't boss me." She couldn't have been more than three at the time and was so tiny that it took all I had to stifle a laugh at the cute little dictator standing in front of me, but she was wildly serious. She did not appreciate being told what to do and when to do it. She had a mind and will of her own, and she planned to use them. My little Lexie Beth was probably all of three feet tall, but she stood her ground like a lion. A little bitty lion.

But I was the boss of her whether she liked it or not. Our relationship was one of God-ordained authority, and even if I hadn't been her mother, I was in every way superior—in weight, size, strength, and wisdom—and I had the ability to enforce my will on her. Like the Lord, however, I had no desire to force my child into compliance. I desperately desired for her to willingly obey, love, and trust me.

Despite the unpopularity of the message that we are in every way inferior to God and should obey Him, it must be shared. God has expectations of us. We are not our own; we were created for a purpose and bought back at a price. He is our Lord. He has every right to rule and have authority over us. Furthermore, He is calling for an extreme obedience that begins with our love.

Recall with me God's command in the Old Testament to his people, Israel, to "love the LORD your God with all your heart and with all your soul and with all your strength" (Deuteronomy 6:5). God did not say, "*Obey Me* with all your heart, *obey Me* with all your soul, *obey Me* with all your strength." Rather, God begins the process of claiming a people as His own by requiring their affection.

Professor Jason DeRouchie explains, "There is no room here for divided affections or allegiance. As Jesus said, 'No one can serve two masters' (Matthew 6:24). If indeed there is one God who stands supremely powerful and valuable (Deuteronomy 6:4), this demands a supreme and total loyalty from you and me, a loyalty that starts with the heart."[1]

I think this means that God is not only after our obedience, but also our affection. He wants us to want Him. Yes, He desires for us to revere him, but the Father also wants us to revel in who He is and the love He shows us.

One commentator explains it as follows in his commentary on Matthew 22:37-40:

> *Aheb*, the Hebrew word for love used in Deuteronomy 6:5, refers primarily to an act of mind and will, the determined care for the welfare of something or someone. It might well include strong emotion, but its distinguishing characteristics were the dedication and commitment of choice. It is the love that recognizes and chooses to follow that which is righteous, noble, and true, regardless of what one's feelings in a matter might be…
>
> To love the Lord with all one's heart…soul, and…mind (Mark's account adds "strength," 12:30) does not express separate and technical definitions of each element of human nature or a compartmentalizing of love into three or four categories, but rather connotes comprehensiveness. We are to love the Lord our God with every part of our being.[2]

When God asked for the totality of the love of his people—heart, soul, and mind—He was not asking for a blind love. "Genuine love of the Lord is intelligent, feeling, willing, and serving. It involves thought, sensitivity, intent, and even action where that is possible and appropriate."[3]

God wants us to obey Him, but we must not miss His command for our complete love and affection that will propel us into motion. Our God is a relational God. In the beginning, before the world began, He was in a loving, committed relationship with the Son and the Spirit. When He created humanity, it was to be in relationship. When sin severed that relationship, God made the first move in love for restoration. "For God so loved the world that he gave his one and only Son, that whoever believes in him shall not perish but have eternal life" (John 3:16).

Jesus modeled for us the most severe discipleship of all by laying down His life in love and submission to the Father for the salvation of others. And when He stood on the mountain before He ascended into heaven, He said, "All authority in heaven and on earth has been given to me. Therefore go and make disciples of all nations, baptizing them in the name of the Father and of the Son and of the Holy Spirit, and teaching them to obey everything I have commanded you" (Matthew 28:18-20).

While God wants our affection, it would be wrong to think that He left us to make up our own minds about morality and how to apply His teachings. Jesus was absolutely clear that He served at the pleasure of the Father, spoke what was directed by Him, and imaged Him to the world. Jesus did not abolish the law but fulfilled it (Matthew 5:17). When He commissioned His followers, He did not say, "Teach people to love Me," but rather, "All authority belongs to Me; disciple people and teach them to obey."

This must be clear in our minds as followers of Christ and as parents: Jesus did not come to set us free *from* obedience; He came to set us free *for* obedience. He did not come so that we could live our lives as if there were no authority but our own and no wisdom higher than our own. He came to free us to love and obey the Father in a way we could never do without His conquering death and the gift of His Spirit inside us.

We have to be taught to love God, and we have to be taught how to obey Jesus. Neither of these things will develop on their own without cultivation. The apostles who gathered on the mountain understood these truths. They were deeply committed to doing the enduring work of building people of faith, character, and strength.

Paradigm Shift

When the apostle Paul met Jesus on the road to Damascus in Acts 9, the paradigm through which he saw the world shifted in an instant. Until that point, Paul had been zealous for the law of Judaism as a Pharisee. He had been raised in a devout Jewish home and must have excelled in his religious classes, because he went to study in Jerusalem at the foot of an esteemed teacher named Gamaliel (Acts 22:3). He loved God and the Scriptures, but the problem was that he didn't recognize the prophecies that pointed to Jesus.

When Paul caught wind that Jesus claimed to be the Messiah and that His followers were perpetuating this "rumor," his passion shifted from religious righteousness to religious extremism, and he began persecuting the early Christian church.

Imagine his shock when the light blinded him and the voice called him by name: "Saul, Saul, why do you persecute me?" (Acts 9:4). The voice was that of Jesus. In that moment, everything Paul thought he knew unwound around him. He sat in the darkness, neither eating nor drinking for three days, waiting (verse 9).

I can only imagine what was going through his mind during that time. *Where did I go wrong? How did I miss this? Wasn't I supposed to defend the faith I love? Will I be punished?*

A man named Ananias came at the direction of the Lord to restore Paul's sight. Ananias was rightfully afraid, for Paul had come to terrorize the believers and throw them into prison. Still, "the Lord said to Ananias, 'Go! This man is my chosen instrument to proclaim my name to the Gentiles and their kings and to the people of Israel. I will show him how much he must suffer for my name'" (verses 15-16).

So the man went to Paul and placed his hands on him—and "scales" fell off the Pharisee's eyes. Paul got up and was baptized in the name of Jesus; he ate and was restored (verses 18-19). "At once he began to preach in the synagogues" (verse 20), but this time he brought a new message. Paul, for the first time in his life, declared the coming of the Messiah, Jesus as the Son of God. The change was astounding.

While the other apostles, all called by God, were devoted, none of them possessed the background of Paul. He had given his life to the study of the law and Jewish Scriptures. We know that among the disciples there were fishermen, a zealot, and a tax collector, but Paul was a rabbi. We can praise God for this, because the responsibility of unpacking Jewish history, laws, promises, prophecy, imagery, and their fulfillment in Christ Jesus fell largely to Paul and Matthew. It is Paul, the converted religious fanatic, whom we owe for our understanding of theology found in the book of Romans. He is the one who wrote the majority of the epistles and conducted numerous missionary journeys that helped take Christianity across racial and religious lines. Paul spent his life masterfully demonstrating that the rescue found in Jesus had been the plan all along.

Among all those who walked with Paul and served beside him, one young man rose to the top. Timothy became Paul's spiritual son, dearly loved by the anointed apostle. Their relationship was deep and gratifying and included world travel without any perks for being frequent fliers. Because they preached Jesus as the crucified and risen Savior, they were assaulted and harassed at almost every stop. Timothy saw his mentor arrested before his eyes. He watched crowds turn to Christ and witnessed crowds turn on Paul. It was to Timothy that Paul wrote about his responsibility to carry on with the work of sharing the gospel and building the church. It was to Timothy that we find these words addressed: "Don't let anyone look down on you because you are young, but set an example for the believers in speech, in conduct, in love, in faith and in purity" (1 Timothy 4:12).

Speech, conduct, love, faith, and purity. They have the air of totality, don't they? Paul gave every part of his being, every ounce of his courage, to the building of the early church. Loving God with all his heart, mind, soul, and strength, he taught Timothy what a life of following Jesus must look like. This life would require Timothy's everything. He was young, but his character was already being shaped by Christ. Timothy's life would be marked in every way by the transforming and redeeming love of Christ—and that love would be demonstrated to the world in how he lived.

The same is true for our kids as we raise and prepare them to stand, lead, and drive the kingdom of God forward in a culture full of selfishness and perversion. Our kids can stand. They can lead. They can be change agents. But it will require totality. They must not rebuff the severity of God's call to discipleship.

Our children need parents who will cheer them on, help them stand when they fall, and wrap them in undying love—yes—but they also need parents who will uphold the standards of God before them. If we flinch and rebuff the totality of love and loyalty to truth and righteousness that the Lord requires, we cannot lead our children in this way.

The call of God to love Him in heart, mind, soul, and strength and the call to set an example in speech, conduct, love, faith, and purity are our first priorities as parents. As Pope Francis said, "Jesus is radical. He *gives all and he asks all*: he gives a love that is total and asks for an undivided heart."[4]

Lord,

May it be so in me. Help me love You with the totality of my mind, heart, soul, and strength. Remove from me the things that are not fitting in my speech, conduct, love, faith, and purity. Help me lead my child along the same path. You are worthy. In Jesus's name, amen.

6

The Case for Character

Teaching the Benefits of Character

> He is rich or poor according to what he *is*, not according to what he *has*.
>
> HENRY WARD BEECHER

B lessing rarely looks like we think it will. It's seldom a rainbow without a thunderstorm or a time of peace without a battle first. When it comes to the journey of building character, God promises to keep His eye upon us and to offer His reward and favor. But nowhere does He say the process will be easy.

Joseph was born into a complicated family. His father, Jacob, had multiple wives and concubines, along with a slew of alpha-male sons. There was already a less-than-friendly rivalry between his mother, Rachel, and his aunt Leah. Joseph was born to Jacob in his old age, and by the time Joseph was old enough to pull his weight in the household, his older brothers were in charge of his father's flocks, likely with families of their own. There was little place in the family shepherding business for a kid brother who was doted on by their father.

Scripture says that Jacob "loved Joseph more than any of his other sons...When his brothers saw that their father loved him more than

any of them, they hated him and could not speak a kind word to him"
(Genesis 37:3-4). The environment in which Joseph grew up was toxic.
His dad made him that famous coat of many colors, a trophy of his
father's love. Joseph wore it—much to the displeasure of his brothers,
because it certainly wasn't a coat fit for men who worked the ground
and tended animals. (Trust me. I'm a farm wife; I know.)

To make matters worse, Joseph had dreams, ones where he was at
the top and his brothers were listening to him. Not just listening, but
bowing down to him.

Should he have shared about the dreams? Who knows. The one
thing we know for sure is that he was 17 years old when the situation
blew up and he had to endure more than any teenager should.

Being sent on an errand to check on his brothers out in the field
would seem harmless. However, Joseph's brothers' anger and jealousy
had crossed a dangerous line. " 'Here comes that dreamer!' they said to
each other. 'Come now, let's kill him and throw him into one of these
cisterns and say that a ferocious animal devoured him. Then we'll see
what comes of his dreams' " (Genesis 37:19-20).

His eldest brother, Reuben, heard this and was filled with concern.
Was he angry at his father and Joseph? Absolutely, but he thought murder was flat wrong. So instead of killing Joseph, the brothers threw him
into an empty hole and callously sat down to eat a meal together.

With their little brother out of sight, they saw a caravan of Ish-
maelites coming, loaded down with goods to sell in Egypt. That was
when Joseph's brother Judah thought of a better plan than murder—
they would sell Joseph into slavery instead and tell their father that he
had died.

Seventeen years old. I have a teenager, so I realize that raising Joseph
probably wasn't peaches and cream, but no one deserves to be abused
and sold into slavery.

His family may have rejected him, but God was squarely on his side
and had planted dreams of the future deep inside him—dreams that
would be fulfilled for God's glory, not Joseph's.

Ease or Blessing?

In Egypt, the favor and eye of the Lord were on Joseph. He was purchased by the captain of Pharaoh's guard, a man named Potiphar.

> The LORD was with Joseph so that he prospered, and he lived in the house of his Egyptian master. When his master saw that the LORD was with him and that the LORD gave him success in everything he did, Joseph found favor in his eyes and became his attendant. Potiphar put him in charge of his household, and he entrusted to his care everything he owned. From the time he put him in charge of his household and of all that he owned, the LORD blessed the household of the Egyptian because of Joseph. The blessing of the LORD was on everything Potiphar had, both in the house and in the field. So Potiphar left everything he had in Joseph's care; with Joseph in charge, he did not concern himself with anything except the food he ate (Genesis 39:2-6).

Joseph may have been rejected by his family, but God's blessing was evident.

However, we must remember that God's favor and call on our lives does not mean we will have everyone's favor. Living a life with a commitment to excellence and integrity does not mean that we will be the most powerful person in the room or that we will win a popularity contest. It does, however, mean that we will have deeper wisdom than we could access on our own, that we will have the confidence and trust of key people involved in the mission we were put on earth to fulfill.

God's blessing doesn't mean a life without labor either. Joseph was not snapping selfies by the Nile and tagging them #Blessed, #WorkHardPlayHarder, or #TakeThisBros.

Joseph stewarded God's blessing and the stages of early manhood with humility and discretion. He grew into a handsome man, which caught the eye of Potiphar's wife. She pursued him to seduce him.

But he refused. "With me in charge," he told her, "my master does not concern himself with anything in the house; everything he owns he has entrusted to my care. No one is greater in this house than I am. My master has withheld nothing from me except you, because you are his wife. How then could I do such a wicked thing and sin against God?" (Genesis 39:8-9).

Even though she pursued Joseph "day after day," he steadfastly refused her (verse 10). Give this kid a medal, folks. But then one day Potiphar's wife grabbed hold of him, and he left his cloak behind and ran. Tell me there isn't some irony in him leaving behind a second cloak to be saved!

False charges were then trumped up against poor Joseph, and he was thrown into Pharaoh's prison. It seems terrible, but here's the thing: He could have been executed for the accusation of assaulting the captain of the guard's wife. I wonder if Joseph's integrity spoke for itself that day. Regardless, Joseph lived but spent years in prison.

> While Joseph was there in the prison, the LORD was with him; he showed him kindness and granted him favor in the eyes of the prison warden. So the warden put Joseph in charge of all those held in the prison, and he was made responsible for all that was done there. The warden paid no attention to anything under Joseph's care, because the LORD was with Joseph and gave him success in whatever he did (Genesis 39:20-23).

Do you sense a pattern? If we buy into the idea that the blessing of God only comes to us in comfortable positions and times of ease, we will miss the opportunity to see the hand of God working through us and our children.

Even in prison, when all was not going Joseph's way, he used his gifts, proved himself trustworthy, and was evidently a pleasure to work with—even though being an unpaid prison warden was scarcely his dream job. And there in prison, the dreamer was used by God to do some dream interpretation, pointing back to God as the knower of dreams (see Genesis 40). Hope rose in Joseph that maybe this would mean the end of his prison sentence. Yet years passed, and he remained.

Until one day God used Joseph to interpret a dream of Pharaoh's that impacted not just Egypt but also all the surrounding nations, including the land of Joseph's family. Not only was Joseph given the wisdom of God to interpret Pharaoh's dream, but he also was given insight into the deliverance plan for hundreds of thousands of people during a time of unprecedented famine. His advice to Pharaoh was simple: "Look for a discerning and wise man and put him in charge of the land of Egypt" (Genesis 41:33).

> Then Pharaoh said to Joseph, "Since God has made all this known to you, there is no one so discerning and wise as you. You shall be in charge of my palace, and all my people are to submit to your orders. Only with respect to the throne will I be greater than you" (verses 39-40).

Joseph was 30 years old when he went from an Egyptian prison to the palace. Time and probably a good feast or two helped ease the memories of the trials and hardships he had endured. He married and had two sons. The first he named Manasseh, "because God has made me forget all my trouble and all my father's household" (verse 51). The second he called Ephraim, saying, "It is because God has made me fruitful in the land of my suffering" (verse 52). Clearly, some pain was not erased by the favor and blessing of the Lord, but Joseph's story demonstrates that there can be healing and redemption.

Joseph's interpretation of Pharaoh's dream came true, and seven years of bumper crops were then followed by seven years of devastating famine. I think about how there was a drought last year on our farm, and we faired okay—but having seven years of drought in a row would cripple not only our farm, but the national economy as well. And that's exactly what happened in Joseph's world.

His brothers headed to Egypt to see if they could find relief from Pharaoh, and in a story that God alone could write, Joseph sat in authority over his brothers. He was given the chance to repay all the evil, all the pain, and all the brokenness they had dished out. Should he throw *them* in a pit, plan *their* murders, sell *them* as slaves, or throw *them* in prison? The possibilities for retribution were endless, and yet, when the moment arose and the background music swelled, Joseph's God-honoring character spoke for itself. He told his brothers, "Don't be afraid. Am I in the place of God? You intended to harm me, but God intended it for good to accomplish what is now being done, the saving of many lives" (Genesis 50:19-20).

Tightly wound into our cultural view of blessing is the idea that when we are blessed, we will live a life of ease. But this is not biblical. We must tell our children that God's favor and blessing over their lives are worth any sacrifice they must make for it.

It is important to note that Joseph's family was the dysfunctional, broken family that God used as the bloodline of not only His people, Israel, but also the Savior. When it came to the brothers' inheritance, Joseph's family received a double portion, as Jacob blessed his sons and allowed Manasseh and Ephraim to become part of the twelve tribes of Israel. We cannot always see the reward for our obedience and faithfulness, but we can know with steadfast certainty that the Father has promised us good.

Good in Jesus

Some of my favorite people in the world live in Port-au-Prince, Haiti. For the last five years, I have led teams of Bible teachers to this impoverished, developing country in the Caribbean Sea. The smiles on the Haitians' faces, the love in their voices, and the way we hug until we have to let go all remind me that heaven will be sweet when we have no more goodbyes.

My friend Nicole is a single mother to a precious boy named Warens. We met on my first trip to Haiti when she came to our conference with a room full of other women's directors from several Haitian churches. I loved teaching Nicole. She absorbed every word, asked questions, and corrected me when something didn't make sense in the Haitian cultural context. I loved watching her learn, particularly when I would make a joke in English and she would laugh before it was translated. She used all her resources to understand and did her homework at night by lantern light. On the final day of the conference we hugged, and I could hardly let go.

Fast-forward through five years, two hurricanes, unemployment, a new job, vast political instability, and the ongoing task of raising her precious son on her own. Through that time God has knit our hearts together like sisters. We text a few times a week and are inseparable when we get together.

In February 2019, Haiti became violent and unstable, and people were unable to leave their homes for fear of being shot or injured. The United States removed all nonessential personnel from the American embassy and issued the highest-level travel advisory. During that time, my friends were unable to leave their homes to find food, to go to school, or even to work. I sat at home nearly in shock as they sent reports of the spiraling crisis they were facing. At one point I finally texted Nicole, "Do you have food and water?" My stomach was in my throat.

"Yes! I have water but I don't have food," she wrote back. "Thank you for your prayers, sister, we need it for peace in Haiti. God bless you more. I love you."

I sobbed. *God bless* me *more?* I wrote back, "I'm on my knees asking God for help, Nicole. I love you."

"Thank you very much, sister. I love you, too."

The next day God worked an absolute miracle. My Haitian friends were allowed outside their homes for relief and food for the first time in ten days. I've talked to Nicole dozens of times when circumstances were good and when circumstances were hard, and her answer to the question, "How are you?" is always the same.

"I'm good in Jesus," she says to me. I scarcely know what to say in reply. She lives in a one-room hut on a hill with little electricity, no bathroom, and no refrigerator, working day and night to take care of her son and serve as the lay secretary of her church and a preschool teacher. And she is blessed. She believes it in her soul, and finally, so do I. Nicole is good in Jesus, and come what may, my family will be too.

The Blessing of a Life of Character

It may be my personality type (ENFP), behavioral style (*I* on the DiSC profile), and pain-avoidant style, but I can't thrive very long in an environment that focuses on rules. Start an experience off with a running list of the things I can't do or must avoid, and I am ready to shut down and go someplace fun. It's not that I don't see the value in setting boundaries; it's just that I would rather celebrate the freedom and fullness of an experience, major on the rewards and benefits, and then set expectations.

When it comes to discussing matters of character, morality, and virtue, it is not a stretch to say that the rewards far outweigh the limitations placed on us by God. There is so much more to character than following rules. There is blessing, pleasure, opportunity, and joy available to the righteous. We don't want to just warn our kids that living a life devoid of character is harmful; rather, we must focus on the rewards available to those who do the hard work of choosing a life of integrity.

So let's unpack the value of a life of character and discuss some practical ways to begin exploring this benefit with your children. The next few pages include six benefits to living a life of character that we can discuss with our kids. Take some time to read the Scriptures I've referenced with your kids and ask for their feedback on what they learn. What does God want them to know? Is there something He wants them to act on or change?

Six Benefits of Living with
Godly Character Lessons

Whenever we engage our children in discussion, it's helpful to ask questions to check for comprehension and to draw a baseline on their understanding. With this understanding of the nuances in their understanding, teaching can be richer and in greater depth. Help them remember times in their lives when they experienced one of these truths at work in the world. Be sure to share your experiences with them too.

1. When you build a life of character, you will be blessed.

The blessing of God is not something that can be described on a license plate frame or scrawled across a T-shirts without watering down its meaning. To have God's favor and blessing over your life is unparalleled in its benefit. This does not mean we will receive financial blessing or promotions in the world, although it could. But we gain an even deeper and richer understanding in the words of Jesus: "Blessed are the poor in spirit, for theirs is the kingdom of heaven. Blessed are those who mourn, for they will be comforted. Blessed are the meek, for they will inherit the earth" (Matthew 5:3-5).

The blessing of God is the divine pleasure and satisfaction of God. But it could also mean the favor of people as well. Children who are well mannered and respectful are trusted with greater responsibilities and more independence. On many occasions, I have watched my kids be given opportunities that many other kids would never have experienced because adults observed their behavior and trusted them to obey. This has meant seeing cool procedures in doctors' offices and getting behind-the-scenes tours in museums, on airplanes, and in government offices. But at the end of the day, there is a personal satisfaction beyond words that comes with living a life of integrity.

Scriptures: 2 Samuel 6:12; Luke 2:52; Ephesians 6:1-3

Questions: Why is it fun to have people like and enjoy you? How do you feel when you make a good choice? What does it mean to have someone's favor?

Activity: Try a role switch between parents and kids, either in an actual activity or just talking through an example. Pretend to go grocery shopping and have the "child" refuse to listen to directions, pull unwanted items off shelves, and wander off. Talk through a trip on an airplane or a visit to a museum. What blessings are there for obeying and listening?

2. When you build a life of character, you will shine.

Our family lives on four acres of grass. If you visited us in the middle of the night, when everything is dark, you would be able to see the tiny light from a birthday candle. The lighting of a candle in a field of darkness is easily seen. Jesus said it would be this way.

> You are the light of the world. A town built on a hill cannot be hidden. Neither do people light a lamp and put it under a bowl. Instead they put it on its stand, and it gives light to everyone in the house. In the same way, let your light shine before others, that they may see your good deeds and glorify your Father in heaven (Matthew 5:14-16).

For better or worse, your commitment to character will draw attention. This can make you quite a witness for Jesus to the people around you. My friend, Jeanna, tells the story of getting two raises in two weeks in a job she had in a retail store. Her work ethic and reliability spoke for themselves, and she was quickly identified by her supervisors as a person on whom they could depend. Because she was surrounded by people who were unreliable, distracted, and immature, Jeanna's faithfulness was noticeable.

Scriptures: John 8:12; Ephesians 5:8-9

Questions: For what do you want to be known? Who are some people you admire and why? How do you see people of character shine in our world?

Activity: Light a small candle in a dark room and pray together, asking God to help others see God's light inside you. Read a biography of a Christian God has used to impact our culture.

3. *When you build a life of character,*
   you will attract good friends.

Proverbs 13:20 explains, "Walk with the wise and become wise, for a companion of fools suffers harm." It was God's idea that we would be swayed by those we walk alongside. Those who walk with character are more likely to draw other people of character to them. As "deep calls to deep" (Psalm 42:7), so righteousness calls to righteousness. It should be with great joy that we explain to our kids that those who choose to walk in integrity are much more likely to experience the reward of having close, loyal companions.

Scriptures: Proverbs 17:17; 27:6,17; Ecclesiastes 4:9-12

Questions: What character qualities do you want your closest friends to have? Do you have a friend who helps you make wise choices and points you to Jesus? If not, could we pray about that right now?

Activity: Grab some magnets to use as an illustration and have a talk about the kind of friends and relationships your kids want to have in their lives. Who are they naturally drawn toward in their friendships? Will these friends point them to Jesus? Are they that kind of friend to others?

4. *When you build a life of character,*
   you will grow in wisdom.

When our hearts are bent toward righteousness, God can more easily lead and guide us, and our hearts are free to listen to Him. Sin clouds our judgment and minds, and while the world celebrates folly and peddles confusion, God gives us the ability to think clearly when the heat is on.

Scriptures: 1 Corinthians 1:30; James 1:5

Questions: What does wisdom mean? What distracts you from making good decisions?

Activity: Have your children try doing an intellectual activity (for example, writing a short story) while listening to loud music or watching a TV show. Then ask them how the distractions affected their ability to write. Did they misspell words they know, forget words from sentences, or miss pieces of the story? Remind them that sin and foolishness can also distract them from thinking clearly.

5. *When you build a life of character,*
   you can live in freedom.

Shame and fear come with living apart from the life God desires for us. People of character don't have to be afraid of lies piling up and covering their tails. Anxiety and stress are diminished for the people who know they have chosen to act with integrity. Not only do these choices bring personal fulfillment, but they can also bring protection from charges against us.

Scriptures: Galatians 5:1,22-23; 1 Peter 2:16

Questions: What does it mean to be in captivity, slavery, or bondage? How is being stuck in sin like being in jail?

Activity: Get an old-fashioned finger trap (also called Chinese handcuffs). Let your children struggle in the trap and feel a metaphor for captivity as well as the relief of freedom, even if they manage to remove it on their own.

6. *When you build a life of character,*
   you can expect a reward.

Even if our children never see the fruit of their good deeds and right living on earth, they can know with certainty that God is keeping track. There will be a reckoning for sin and righteousness because our God is just and faithful. It's difficult for us to grasp a long wait for a blessing we cannot wrap our hands around, but our children will learn as we talk about that reality.

Scriptures: Proverbs 3:5-6; Lamentations 3:25; 1 Peter 5:2-4

Questions: Can you remember a time when you had to wait a long while for something? What kinds of things are worth waiting for? Why should we wait for rewards?

Activity: Grab snack-size candy bars and hand one to each of your children at breakfast time. Tell them that the candy is theirs—but at the end of the day, if they still haven't opened it, you'll have a reward for them. Don't tell them what that reward will be! At the end of the day, ask them for the small candy bar. If they have it, reward them with a giant candy bar and explain to them that God has big rewards in store for us when we live His way. Those rewards may not be seen in their lifetimes, but Hebrews 11 is filled with people who lived without seeing the fruit of their faith. God saw and rewarded their faithfulness, and He sees ours too!

> *Father,*
>
> *You are the giver of every good and perfect gift, including my Savior, Jesus. Help me to see blessing and favor through Your eyes and to train my child to value Your favor. What a gift it would be for him to grow up in the center of Your will, with Your hand upon him. Father, please give him wisdom and discernment and a sense of gratitude for Your hand on his life. In Jesus's name, amen.*

7

Moral Compass

Conscience and the Holy Spirit

> We may get our moral bearings by looking at
> God. We must begin with God. We are right
> when, and only when, we stand in a right position
> relative to God, and we are wrong so far and
> so long as we stand in any other position.
>
> A.W. TOZER

I'm a natural navigator. I don't know if this skill developed because my dad is a retired lieutenant colonel and he drilled it into me, or because we grew up traveling, or because God simply knew I would need this gift. Regardless, no matter my location, I tend to be a quick study when it comes to learning how to navigate my surroundings.

When I was growing up in the foothills of Colorado, it was simple to know which direction I was facing. The mountains, when we were at home in Colorado Springs, were always to the west. Naturally, that meant that the way to Denver was north and the way to the base where my dad worked was south. Finding my way back home simply meant lifting my eyes to the hills.

When I moved to attend college at Moody Bible Institute in

downtown Chicago, my navigational bearings were reoriented. At any place downtown, I could look for the Sears Tower (currently called the Willis Tower) by the river, to the south of Moody. The John Hancock Center sat two blocks to the north and six blocks to the east of Moody on Michigan Avenue. If I kept heading east, I'd run right into Lake Shore Drive and Lake Michigan.

This may sound confusing if Chicago isn't your city. However, my husband, Mike, and I take our family to Chicago several times a year and have allowed our kids to navigate us around town on buses, trains, and by foot as early as they were able to walk while holding our hands. We have merely taught them to look up and be confident in their ability to read the building markers around them.

When I moved to Chicago for school, I recognized that my ability to navigate was going to take some fine-tuning when surveying the hills and horizon were no longer an option. Then when Mike and I got married, we moved to his hometown in rural West Michigan, which had a population of 2,000. The directions I got there might well have been given in Greek. They would begin with something like, "Head up the road, and when you come to a T in front of the Mouls', take a right. At the dirt road take a left. The Brethren schoolhouse will be on the right. Two apple blocks up on the right, before the new cherries, is a dirt path. Follow it up, and at the back of the old Moul farm he's working." Sure.

These directions required knowledge of a family and their old farm from the back side, a schoolhouse that is actually a modular, and whether or not an out-of-season tree would bear apples or cherries. When that failed—and believe me, it did—people would say, "Head east. At the T, take a right and head south. At the dirt road, turn east…" This was all before we had dashboards in our cars with built-in compasses.

I was often advised that I would know the directions with only one bearing, one landmark: Lake Michigan was west. Always west. This assumed that I had "Lake-dar," similar to radar, and was able to discern someone's location based on something I could not always see. I'm happy to announce that 13 years into living here for the second time, I have achieved basic "Lake-dar" skills.

We are now navigating a world that is spinning more quickly. Boundaries and markings that have helped us find our way morally in the past have now been blurred or compromised. The words we once viewed as uncivil and inappropriate not only appear on cable television and evening prime time but also hit the morning news in regular sound bites. Leadership positions we once esteemed, whether in the government or in church, are now viewed with skepticism at best and distrust and malice at worst. Don't get me wrong; our society never had it all right. But on both sides of the political aisle, perhaps we've never been so wrong.

This, of course, leaves us parenting breathless, often uncertain of the path before us.

This past week my sister, Casey, called and asked me if I knew what her son would be learning in health class that day. Tongue in cheek, I asked, "Is it the banana and condom lesson?" I vividly remembered that day in my own health class, including how a bottle of contraceptive foam had exploded during the talk.

She said, "No, today they are discussing how to have protected anal sex and safe homosexual behavior. Yesterday they discussed oral sex."

I sucked in a breath. "What are you going to do?" I asked.

"Well, I was able to see the curriculum before they began, and we've already had several conversations with him. We decided not to pull him out of the class for this unit. We'd rather his friends not regurgitate the lessons to him with false information, because you know they will. Each night I'm trying to make sure that we talk to him about what he learned that day and recalibrate with truth."

This is the kind of situation we face every single day as parents in a world with shades of gray and newsfeeds full of ambiguity, half-truths, or plain and simple deception. How will you navigate parenting your children in this evolving generation? How will you teach them to navigate as they let go of your hand and begin the next season without you holding on to them? How do you determine whether the issue you face today is a hard-and-fast line that a child of God must not cross or a place for Christian liberty?

Find North

The psalmist once asked a similar question: "How can a young person stay on the path of purity?" (Psalm 119:9). It's comforting to know that this question has been asked in countless generations before ours. Parents and leaders have stared at the culture around them and wondered how the kids they loved could walk through this minefield of life without being maimed and devastated. Fortunately for us, our God-inspired psalmist also penned the answer.

"How can a young person stay on the path of purity? *By living according to your word*" (Psalm 119:9, emphasis added). Our kids will only be able to successfully navigate the world in this way—with faith in Christ Jesus, the Holy Spirit inside them, and every step taken according to the Word of God. The psalmist continues by describing how he is practicing his own godly navigating.

> I seek you with all my heart;
>> do not let me stray from your commands.
> I have hidden your word in my heart
>> that I might not sin against you.
> Praise be to you, LORD;
>> teach me your decrees.
> With my lips I recount
>> all the laws that come from your mouth.
> I rejoice in following your statutes
>> as one rejoices in great riches.
> I meditate on your precepts
>> and consider your ways.
> I delight in your decrees;
>> I will not neglect your word (Psalm 119:10-16).

Our children's greatest need is a relationship with Jesus. Until they come to Christ, they cannot find true north in this world. He is the changeless mark on the horizon in every generation. Christ is the pathway to godliness, and imitating Jesus and imaging Him to the world is the goal. The Holy Spirit is our guide who continually points us to Christ and redirects us, and God's Word is the daily map that keeps us out of the ditch.

We train our children to walk in character, purity, and holiness by using the Word to lead them. Is Scripture the framework from which you are rearing your children? Are you constantly pointing them back to the Word of God as a guide for each step? Are you seeking answers together, or are you training them to lean on you or their own understanding? Proverbs 3:5-7 is clear about this pitfall: "Trust in the LORD with all your heart and lean not on you own understanding; in all your ways submit to him, and he will make your paths straight. Do not be wise in your own eyes; fear the LORD and shun evil."

Countercultural parents must be saturated in the Word so they know how to direct their children. It is not unusual for me to be approached by a woman after an event who says, "I'm new to this. I love Jesus, but I don't know how to read my Bible. I don't know how to pray it, and I don't know how to use it in my childrearing."

I see the fear and concern in her eyes, and I often hug her and say, "You only need to be one step ahead of them right now. Let's figure this out together."

In the back of this book you'll find some of my favorite resources for learning how to study the Word and use it in your parenting. It's absolutely okay to be a beginner. But it's not okay to stay stuck.

The apostle Paul wrote the following words to Timothy, whom he called his "beloved child" (2 Timothy 1:2 ESV):

> As for you, continue in what you have learned and have become convinced of, because you know those from whom you learned it, and how from infancy you have known the

> Holy Scriptures, which are able to make you wise for salvation through faith in Christ Jesus. All Scripture is God-breathed and is useful for teaching, rebuking, correcting and training in righteousness, so that the servant of God may be thoroughly equipped for every good work (2 Timothy 3:14-17).

Timothy was blessed to have a grandmother and mother who taught him the Scriptures from a very young age (see also 2 Timothy 1:5). Timothy likely sat at their knee and on their laps and learned the Word and how to love God.

Children become trained and "convinced" because they trust us. They see our love, our way of life, and they rely on our experiential knowledge of the Lord until they form their own. Eventually they can believe for themselves, but all along the way we must weave the Word that we have learned and studied into their days. We must remind them that Christ is relevant in every little thing. We must teach them God's ways and His laws.

Friend, is God's Word your guide for life? Do you seek wisdom found in the Word? Do you lay your head down on top of your open Bible and say, "I don't know how to do this; show me?" God honors those prayers. He knows our needs and promises to give us wisdom generously (see James 1:5).

Turn Down the Noise

We are now parenting the most connected generation ever to walk the planet. We have resources at our fingertips that make our job of parenting easier and our kids' lives richer. Just this week, I've used an app on my phone to log driver-training hours, research a health concern, check my kid's missing assignments, and pray for my children. I can't imagine trying to check my daughter's sixth grade English papers without a sentence-diagramming website open, and I'm a writer! I relish the notifications from the school reminding me of parent-teacher conferences. I love being able to watch basketball layup and knot-tying demonstrations on YouTube.

But these gifts are not without cost. Rarely ten minutes go by without hearing a phone vibrate across the room. The buzz and stream of information to our families is constant and deafening. The pull on our children (and us, if we are honest) is tremendous. We live in an "on demand" generation, and it has never been noisier.

As parents, we have to put our foot down and stop the noise so our families have the opportunity to hear from the Lord. That begins with us. We need to silence our phones and model for our children a time of listening. I won't prescribe what that will look like for you, but for me it has meant waking up before my kids as often as I am able in order to spend time with the Bible open on my lap and a prayer journal beside me, intentionally quieting myself so I can hear. For my husband, Mike, it sometimes means quiet mornings but more often means quiet moments during his lunch hour, or in a tractor, or on long walks in the woods. When our requests (and sometimes demands) for our kids to shut down the technology are met with resistance, it is much easier to make a case for its worthiness if we already have the habit built into our own lives.

Make no mistake, people are planning how to influence our children. Advertisers, politicians, musicians, and entertainment specialists are all planning ways to capture our affection. God rarely gets our attention by shining a spotlight into our eyes. He works in the small, often quiet moments, and if we are going to help our families detect His leadership and direction in their lives, we may have to turn off their devices for them. In our home, having a "quiet time," also known as reading Scripture, is on our children's list of daily responsibilities.

When Brendan, my oldest, was a baby, I would nestle him in my arms and read him a toddler's Bible storybook and pray over him like he could understand every word. As he became a squirmy toddler, this time became less quiet. The Bible readings became more animated, and I gave him an opportunity to fill in our prayers with requests and thank-yous.

When Brendan became an early reader, we found another Bible for kids. As soon as he woke up, he would bring out his Bible and sit on the couch with me in the mornings, sounding out words beside me. That's when the questions began—ones I asked and ones I received. By this point our family had grown to four, and my hands were full trying to create an environment where each of my children had an opportunity to learn and meet with the Lord.

Some days and months this intentionality felt like an uphill battle. However, I look back and am so glad for those little moments of sowing into my kids. Now when I ask them if they have read their Bibles, they don't roll their eyes or disregard the request, because they see that time as vital.

We as parents create this environment by prioritizing it. That means spending time in Scripture takes priority over other things, and we do it even when we are worn bare and worn out—because our kids are going to need to know how to seek the Lord on their own. This is all about creating a beaten-down path to the Father for them so they know the way to go when the Lord calls.

Recognize God's Voice

It might seem idyllic to think of parents who started praying and training in the faith before their kids were born. Perhaps you feel late to the party, like you are on a treadmill and are already two steps behind, aware of the distinct possibility of hitting the wall behind you and scuffing up your chin. But know this: Our God is the God of multiple chances, and He's ready to be unleashed in the life of your family. In order for that to happen, though, you may have to make some new habits for your family. Is it okay to require your children to spend time in God's Word? I think so.

If our mission is to train our children to align their lives with the Father and to live in step with the Spirit, how do we teach them to detect His direction in their lives? God longs to be in relationship with

His children and desires for us to recognize His leading. Jesus told us that "whoever belongs to God hears what God says" (John 8:47). This means that today, in our fast-paced society, God is still trying to communicate with His children. The words He speaks to our kids' hearts as they read Scripture and spend time in prayer will be important for the mission they will fulfill during their time on this earth.

Naturally, when we talk about God speaking to us, fear flags start to fly. We have seen the claim of divine inspiration abused, and it is okay for us to feel leery when we hear someone say they've heard from God. However, we must not cast aside the reality of a God who wants to lead His own. It is essential that our children learn to discern His voice in order to fulfill His call on their lives in both the small and big things He has planned. But many of us don't know how to do this for ourselves, so how can we train our children? Let's outline some parameters that will help us form a framework.

God's voice will always speak truth.

God cannot lie. An essential part of His character is his unwavering commitment to truth. "He who is the Glory of Israel does not lie or change his mind; for he is not a human being, that he should change his mind" (1 Samuel 15:29). If at any time He chose to lie or deceive us, that would negate all of His promises; it would shatter His character just as falsehood and deception destroy ours.

This means that if there is a nudging in our hearts or minds to in any way deceive another or cover over the truth, that voice is not from God. Similarly, if we have feelings or leanings that run contrary to Scripture, that is not from God.

The enemy of our souls, Satan, is a liar. Jesus said of the devil that "he was a murderer from the beginning, not holding to the truth, for there is no truth in him. When he lies, he speaks his native language, for he is a liar and the father of lies" (John 8:44). However, we would be mistaken to think it will always be easy to recognize the truth from the lies Satan spews. In his deception of Eve, he asked her if God had really said, "You must not eat from any tree in the garden" (Genesis 3:1). Notice that this was a huge exaggeration of God's prohibition of a singular tree in the garden (see Genesis 2:16-17).

Isn't that like the enemy to take something God said would harm us and twist it into something even more confining? Satan loves to convince us that God's way is harmful and restrictive and leaves us missing out.

This assault on God's character happened again with Jesus. Jesus, "full of the Holy Spirit" (Luke 4:1), was led by the Spirit into the desert to be tempted by the devil. Jesus became depleted from fasting for 40 days and was not delivered from the hunger and pain involved in such a lengthy fast. Then He was approached by the enemy.

The first two temptations were a rather straightforward testing for our Savior. It was easy for Jesus to identify the deception and overcome it with the Word of God, the source of all truth. However, during the final temptation, the enemy upped his game and used Scripture, removed from the context of their situation.

This is where discerning the truth becomes vital.

God's voice will never lead you into sin.

The voice of God will never, ever lead us into sin. He will always lead us to places of love toward Himself and others. His voice calls us into deeper obedience. James says it this way:

> When tempted, no one should say, "God is tempting me." For God cannot be tempted by evil, nor does he tempt anyone; but each person is tempted when they are dragged away by their own evil desire and enticed. Then, after desire has conceived, it gives birth to sin; and sin, when it is full-grown, gives birth to death. Don't be deceived, my dear brothers and sisters (James 1:13-16).

This means that if we are being tempted to disobey God, that leading is not from Him. The enemy is the one who tempts us to disobey, convincing us that we will be most satisfied if we devise our own plan and path. It is our own desires that lead us astray, certainly not God's will for our lives.

God's voice will be good, honorable, and life giving.

We need to teach our children that "every good and perfect gift is from above, coming down from the Father of the heavenly lights, who does not change like shifting shadows. He chose to give us birth through the word of truth" (James 1:17-18). We need to help them identify God as the source of every good thing. That includes their thoughts that align with goodness, honor, and life.

One practical way to do this is to ask our kids what they think should be done in a given situation. If their thoughts, words, and actions align with truth and goodness, we need to help them identify that their response sounds like Jesus.

"Ryan, when you said that your sister must be tired after track practice and that we should be quiet, that sounded a lot like Jesus. I'm so glad that you are thinking His way. Way to go, buddy."

"Brendan, I know you are angry with me, but I see you restraining that anger inside you. I'm proud of you. I know it is hard for us to be respectful to each other when we disagree. I see you looking a lot like Jesus right now. Thank you."

"Gabi, I know it takes courage for you to talk about Jesus with your friends. It must be Him working through you to do that! I see Jesus in you, sweetness. Way to go."

"Lexie Beth, I know that this decision is difficult and you are struggling to make it. I see you asking yourself, 'What is wise in this situation, and what should I do?' I'm grateful you are taking the time to reflect, and I hope you are asking the Lord. That voice inside you that is looking for what is best, that sounds a lot like the voice of wisdom, and that's awesome."

God's voice will honor God and bring Him glory.

The role of the Son is to bring glory to the Father, and the role of the Spirit is to bring glory to both. They aren't alone in that mission. God reveals to us in the book of Isaiah that we were created by Him for His glory and to bring Him praise (43:7,21). Very practically, we will know the voice of truth is speaking in our lives when we find ourselves asking, "Does this honor God?" or "How will this choice bring Him glory?" At other times He may sound a warning to us that we are headed down a path that will not draw us into a closer relationship with Him or bring Him glory.

The best way we can help our kids develop this sense is to teach them their general purpose—to bring glory to God—and then ask them if what they are doing brings Him glory. I do this in my home with a silly game, devoid of cliché answers, and ask my children to play along. "Does eating bring glory to God? How about unloading the dishwasher? What about taking a bath or feeding the cat?" Everything we do becomes fair game, and the more absurd the better.

Maybe you could ask your kids to do a "glory cheer" when they see their brother or sister make a choice that brings glory to God. The goal is to help them see that it's not just the acts we consider "spiritual"— reading our Bibles, praying, attending church, memorizing Scripture— but nearly *everything* has potential to bring God glory. It is all in how we do it. As Paul says, "Whatever you do, whether in word or deed, do it all in the name of the Lord Jesus, giving thanks to God the Father through him" (Colossians 3:17). As parents, we have the privilege to point out to our children God's invitation to participate in every area of their lives.

God's voice will align with the Word of God.

God does not abandon His Word. His Word accomplishes exactly what He desires (Isaiah 55:11), and it remains true across generations. If we sense a stirring inside us that is contrary to God's revealed word to us as found in the Bible, we can know that this is not from the Lord.

My heart is heavy thinking of the number of times I have seen homes shattered by a family member who walked away, believing that

God called them to be "happy" rather than faithful. Equally devastating is the lie that resisting temptation has become "too much" and can't be fought any longer. Friend, both of these ideas do not align with the Word. The truth is that God does not call us to happiness—He invites us into the joy that comes through obedience. He is faithful to be present with us in our suffering and our temptation so that neither will consume us. As Paul writes,

> No temptation has overtaken you except what is common to mankind. And God is faithful; he will not let you be tempted beyond what you can bear. But when you are tempted, he will also provide a way out so that you can endure it (1 Corinthians 10:13).

But in order to know if our feelings and decisions align with the truth of the Word of God, we must know the Word.

What Is a Conscience?

Have you seen a cartoon version of the conscience? On one shoulder rests a little red devil with a pitchfork who whispers terrible ideas, and on the other shoulder rests a little angel in a robe who reminds the individual to act in a way that is kind. Let's also remember Jiminy Cricket from Disney's *Pinocchio*, who is always good but easily forgotten. I don't think either of these cartoon images really do justice to the idea of a conscience.

J.I. Packer writes,

> Conscience is largely autonomous in its operation; though sometimes we can suppress or stifle it, it normally speaks independently of our will, and sometimes, indeed, contrary to our will. And when it speaks, it is in a strange way distinct from us; it stands over us, addressing us with an absoluteness of authority which we did not give it and

which we cannot take from it. To personify conscience and treat it as God's watchman and spokesman in the soul is not, therefore, a mere flight of fancy, it is a necessity of human experience.[1]

God reveals to us in the book of Romans that when He created humankind, He hardwired us with a capacity to know Him and gave us a conscience, this "watchman" that Packer describes. The conscience is a gift from God that holds within it enough good sense to inform every person that there is a moral code and a Creator of that code who intends to be obeyed (Romans 2:15).

In Greek, the original language of the New Testament, the word we translate as *conscience* is *suneidēsis*, a term that means "co-knowledge."[2] Our God-given conscience shows two paths in front of every decision, opportunity, or encounter. One path is morally wholesome, good, and right, while the other is self-centered, negative, and often evil in nature. Before we come to know Christ, our conscience is primitive. It has a general, undeveloped sense of morality that has not yielded to the magnetic pull of Christ.

The conscience also holds a degree of strength. Scripture teaches that it is possible for believers to have a weak conscience that has been untrained (1 Corinthians 8:10,12). Likewise, when we listen to our conscience and obey the voice of truth, we can see our conscience grow in strength. Our conscience can also be seared, or deadened, by disobedience (1 Timothy 4:2), causing us to lose sensitivity to its voice and rendering it less permeable to conviction by the Holy Spirit.

Gray Matters

Recently, my pastor delivered a message that our family has come to refer to as the "weed" message. The sermon was titled, "Clear Thinking on Legal Marijuana," and our pastor began his sermon with these words:

I am a Christian who believes that God is absolute truth and His Word proclaims truth to every area of life. As Christians living out our faith here on planet Earth, there are gray areas that we need to wrestle through under the guidance of God's Word. The older I got, and the more I learned about sexuality, relationships, science, history, politics, drugs, and the Bible, the more I saw these gray areas. I believe to earnestly seek God is to honestly and fearlessly look at the gray and at the relevant issues that are impacting the culture we live in from a biblical perspective.

I'd love to regurgitate for you so much of what my pastor and dear friend said, but I hope you'll settle for this takeaway. It is easier to discern right and wrong when there is a law that specifically says something is out of bounds for our lives. Here in Michigan, when marijuana could only be used medicinally under the direction of a doctor, it was easy to look at our kids and tell them that using weed was wrong. However, now that marijuana has been legalized for adults, we parents have to find a reason beyond "because we said so" when teaching our kids to abstain from drugs in the future.

Our pastor helped us draw some pretty serious conditions for our behavior in general, not just regarding the use of marijuana. He pointed us to 1 Peter 1:13-16 and 1 Thessalonians 5:8 (go read them!), and he said we need to continually ask ourselves these questions:

1. Can I think clearly and be sober minded?
2. Am I exercising self-control so I can live in freedom without bondage?
3. Am I focused on eternal things?
4. Am I acting like a child of God?
5. Is this what someone who is set apart (holy) would do?
6. Is this choice life giving to others, or could this steal life from them?

It would be easier to just be handed the answers rather than having to do the work of praying, studying, and examining our motives, wouldn't it? I came to my own conclusion about the marijuana matter based on statistics and reading the Word, not on society's current popular opinion. We all will face issues as families that fit somewhere between the lines of what is permissible and what is best (see 1 Corinthians 10:23). In these gray matters and all others, God has given us a resource to use in the person of the Holy Spirit.

How Are the Voice of God and the Conscience Different?

Hear this loud and clear: It is a general grace that we have been given a conscience from God, but until we come to know Christ, we are not indwelt with the Holy Spirit. Until our children come to Christ, their moral training and consciences are their only guides in this world. Again, this is why there is no more desperate need in our children's lives than that they come to know Jesus as their Savior.

The human conscience is fallible, but the Holy Spirit is not. We can quench the Spirit's voice through disobedience, making it more difficult to hear Him, but we can never reshape the truth He speaks. Not so with our conscience. Paul spends time in 1 Corinthians talking about how people can train their consciences to flag issues God is not concerned about, while blowing off sins He wants us to stop.

When we look at our world today, we need to look through this lens: People either have the guidance of the Spirit or they are navigating alone. There is no neutral space here. The students who act out in class beside my child do not have the gift of the Spirit. They are flying with consciences that have been impacted by their upbringing, the marks of their previous choices, and the examples of others.

This knowledge changes the way I view disruptions and the brokenness in students and adults around me. It compels me to share the gospel with others and to equip my kids to do the same. These broken kids and adults need what we have, and the only way for them to find it is through exposure to the light inside us. The plan for reaching the world for Christ has remained the same for more than 2,000 years: one person reaching another person, and that person reaching another. These are the words you and I must speak over our kids. We know the way; we have a guide and map. Now let's go practice using them together, until it's time for our kids to journey the next mile without us.

Father,

I am filled with so much gratitude for the gift of Jesus and the Holy Spirit. Thank You that You have not left me here on earth to navigate alone. Thank You for the gift of Your Word in my life. Thank You that it contains everything I need for guidance and direction as I parent my children, and thank You that it also holds everything my children need to walk on the path of righteousness. Point us toward Your heart, Father, and help us bring others along. In Jesus's name, amen.

8

Warring on Your Knees

Praying for Character

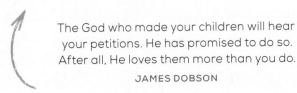

The God who made your children will hear
your petitions. He has promised to do so.
After all, He loves them more than you do.

JAMES DOBSON

My sister, Casey, went through a time of outright rebellion. We all knew it. Her choices and attitude were poor, and the last thing in the world she wanted was to be told what to do. She was halfway through college and certainly didn't want her big sister telling her that her behavior was crazy. Our conversations became short and curt. So I wasn't surprised one day when I turned to her and said, "Casey, I am praying for you," and she made a snooty face and replied, "*Stop* praying for me!" I couldn't help myself—I put my hands on my hips, looked her right in the eye, and said, "Make me."

Prayer is the greatest weapon and tool we have available to us in our parenting journey. In God's incredible mercy, we do not parent alone. The God of the universe is intimately familiar with the ways and workings of our families and has lovingly chosen to make Himself accessible to us. Unfortunately, however, we too often take this information for granted, forget it, or simply choose not to focus our efforts on the privilege of having an ever-present, all-powerful God listening when we cry out.

The Right to Intercede

You are a "priest" in your home. Sound like a stretch? It shouldn't, because you have been given the right and responsibility to go before the Lord on behalf of your family and intercede for their needs. First Peter 2:9 tell us that when we are in Christ, we "are a chosen people, a royal priesthood, a holy nation, God's special possession, that you may declare the praises of him who called you out of darkness into his wonderful light." I don't know how many times I have glossed over the part of that verse that says we are priests, but I found out not too long ago that there is incredible meaning in that role.

Our ability to stand in a place of intercession between God and others is a blood-bought right for us. Before Jesus's death and resurrection, we would not have been given access to an intimate place with the Father. However, at the time of Jesus's death, the veil between God and man was removed. If you are in Christ, you can enter God's presence with assurance and confidence, knowing that you will find grace and help in your time of need (Hebrews 4:16).

At the risk of sounding cliché, God doesn't have "working hours" or times when He is tied up. This means that when our kids fail to come home at curfew, or we catch them vaping, or we see deep cuts on their wrists from self-harm, He can get us right in for a consultation and time of comfort. He is the wisest. He knows what to do. He has parented through this situation before, and He's willing to give you what you need without coercion.

The Responsibility to Intercede

I tell women throughout the nation that I am praying for their children. I work for Moms in Prayer International, a nonprofit whose mission is to reach children and schools for Christ around the world by gathering mothers to pray. Moms in Prayer is in all 50 states and 146 countries, and we take the responsibility of prayer very seriously. So when I look a mother in the eye and say that we are praying for her kid, I do so with integrity. However, no organization can pray with the sincerity, love, detail, and discernment that parents can. No one knows your child like you do.

When my son Brendan was younger, I remember memorizing every little part of him. By the end of his second summer, I had rubbed sunscreen over his tiny back enough times that I noticed when a new freckle formed. Parents are like that. Our kids only need to speak a few words for us to recognize that something is off in their countenance or maybe even their development. This intimacy of relationship makes us the perfect candidates to pray and intercede for our children.

Sometimes, though, we have this knowledge and the burden to pray, but we just don't know where to begin. I don't know how many times I've dropped my head into my hands and whispered to the Lord, "I don't know how to do this." Honesty is a vital component of our relationship with the Lord.

Are you struggling in your role as intercessor for your kids? How and why? It's time to be honest with the Lord about your situation. See if any of these prayers find a spot in your heart, and feel free to turn them into a springboard for prayers of your own.

Feelings of Inadequacy

> *Father, I need You to know that I feel completely inadequate for the job of parenting this child. I'm in over my head, and I don't know what to do. You say in Your Word, in 2 Corinthians 12:9, that Your strength is made sufficient for me and is actually made perfect in my weakness. I invite You to come work and have Your way in our home.*

Feelings of Failure

> *Lord, I've blown it. In my own understanding it seems like I*

have failed my children and You. I can hardly lift my head when I look at _____ [name the situation]. When I _____ [name your part in the failure], I failed to seek Your guidance or act in Your strength and the wisdom You supply. Please forgive me. I invite You and implore You to take this situation and make beauty from it.

Feelings of Shame

Jesus, when I consider the glory that You deserve and the way I have acted in the past in these ways [name the areas that hold feelings of shame], I feel ashamed. I know that shame is not from You but the enemy—and I have no desire to cooperate with him. Please forgive me and help me live in a new space of grace, bringing Your refreshing light into the corners of our family.

Feelings of Apathy

Lord Jesus, You see and know how tired and apathetic I have become in _____ [name the areas where you are failing to discipline, train, and equip your child]. Instead of taking appropriate responsibility for training my child, I have chosen to _____ [confess what has filled your time and what you have occupied yourself with instead of training your child]. Lord, would You renew in me a desire to take every opportunity to win and train my child? I surrender these preoccupations to You and ask You to forgive me for choosing lesser things. You have my attention; please redirect me.

Feeling of Excessive Ownership

God, You know that I have become overinvolved in the life of my child. Instead of turning to You with my fear and concern, I have taken matters into my own hands. I've done this when I _____ [name ways you have tried to *control situations or people rather than trust God]. This is hurting my child because _____ [tell God the ways this is harming your child]. Forgive me, Father. I give my child to You and ask that You prompt my heart when I move toward controlling behavior.*

Feelings of Pride

Lord, I have taken credit for the work You are doing in _____ [your child's name] and in their _____ [name their skills or personality traits in which you have felt pride]. It is right for me to feel joy when they succeed and choose You, Lord, and when they have Your favor over their lives. But when I find my worth swelling or diminishing during their victories and defeats, I know I have placed too much value on these things. Forgive me for drawing my identity and self-worth from anything less than being Your child.

Ask for What You Want

Jesus invited us to be fervent in our prayers and to be confident that we will receive the answers. "If you remain in me and my words remain in you, ask whatever you wish, and it will be done for you" (John 15:7). The apostle John gives us a little more information that adds clarity. "This is the confidence we have in approaching God: that if we ask anything according to his will, he hears us. And if we know that he hears us—whatever we ask—we know that we have what we asked of him" (1 John 5:14-15).

I can recall several times over the course of my parenting journey when one of my kids told me they wanted to ask me for something, and they wanted me to say yes. The problem was I had no idea what was coming or if I could even meet that request. Not so with the heavenly Father. He knows our needs before they are on our tongues, and He knows our thoughts completely. His promise to answer is released when we pray according to His will.

I wish I could look you in the eye as I say this: It is according to God's will that you ask for your children to grow and develop godly character. These are prayers we should boldly and confidently pray, believing with every ounce of our body that God wants to work in our children's lives as much as—and more than—we want Him to do so.

How about starting right here, right now, and praying for your children to have these 20 godly character traits? Dog-ear this page and continue to pray for these things to grow in their lives.

faithfulness (Hebrews 11:1; Proverbs 3:3-4)

obedience (Ephesians 6:1-3)

compassion (Colossians 3:12)

gratefulness (Psalm 9:1)

contentment (Hebrews 13:5)

patience (James 1:19)

discretion (Proverbs 19:11)

self-control (2 Peter 1:5-9)

love (1 Peter 4:8)

truthfulness (Ephesians 4:15)

sexual purity (1 Thessalonians 4:3-7)

humility (James 4:6)

impartiality (James 2:1)

gentleness (Philippians 4:5)

mercy (James 2:13)

kindness (Galatians 5:22)

openness to instruction (Proverbs 9:9)

forgiveness (Ephesians 4:32)

generosity (2 Corinthians 9:7)

joyfulness (Romans 12:12)

Start with one. Write the verse and character trait on a notecard and carry it around with you. Make it a prayer. Spend a day or a week on it and pray for each person in your home. Just start!

Control Issues

If there is one area where a controlling nature will manifest inside us, it's our parenting. True, fervent, trusting prayer forces us to take our grubby hands off the control button of our kids' lives and hand the keys over to the Lord.

Friend, we are going to have to wrestle to the ground the idea that prayer is passive. Prayer is anything *but* passive. When there is nothing left to do but pray, when all our strength has been spent and every option exhausted in the lives of our children, we will finally begin to realize that we have just tapped into the limitless power of our God. He is relentless on our behalf, but His requirement is that we trust Him.

Throughout Scripture, God shows that He delivers His children in the most unconventional ways. It's almost as if He delights in us marveling and saying, "I never saw that coming. I could never have imagined." God loves to blow our minds, delight us, and deliver us with a strong hand.

Want to take a giant leap forward in your faith? Start by praying, "Your will be done," in the area that is breaking your heart, driving you crazy, or scaring you to death. This is a powerhouse prayer to be sure and not for the faint of heart. At the core of those four words, you're saying, "Not my will, Lord, where my kids are happy, well behaved, educated, favored, popular all-stars. But rather, Your will be done in their lives, come what may." I say, "Come what may," because this is not a safe God to whom we are relinquishing our will and children. When we pray like this, we come face to face with a God we cannot control. He will not be bossed by us, we cannot manipulate Him, and our only certainty at the end of the day is the promise that He is working for the good of those who love Him.

Again, God is working for the good way—not the easiest way, and certainly not the path of least resistance. It can be so scary to trust the guide we cannot control, the One who doesn't need our advice when it comes to our children and their futures. What would it look like to take your hands off the controls of your children's lives and place your complete trust in the heavenly Father, believing that He will accomplish the best in your children? What do you need to entrust to Him today?

In Prayer, We Rise

Hannah's heart was broken and becoming bitter. When we meet her on the pages of 1 Samuel, she's childless, *barren*. Could there be a more depressing word? *Barren* aches. It means that someone has longed for something, needed something, searched for something, and come up dry. For Hannah, this drought affected her womb, but it could have been a relational drought, a financial drought, or an emotional drought while watching a child run in the opposite direction from where they should go.

Perhaps, like Hannah, you've cried until there are no more tears and waited. Waited for so, so long for God to move something. Provide something. Maybe, maybe just a drop of hope.

Hannah's situation is different from ours in that she had a sister wife, which we can all agree is a horrible idea. In this case, Hannah's husband's other wife had children and taunted childless Hannah.

I've never been taunted by a sister wife, but I have been taunted by emotions as I've looked at other families. I bet it has happened to you too. It happens in the sandbox as we watch other children's development and good behavior compared to that of our kids. It happens at the fifth-grade band concerts. It happens in the bleachers and at graduation. It happens at church on Sunday mornings. It happens when our kids are rebellious, angry, and withdrawn, and we think of the well-behaved kids in other families. We size up our own family and find ourselves wanting, needing, and sometimes absolutely barren.

But Hannah made a pivotal choice in the middle of her barren season that changed everything. She rose and went before the Lord.

> After they had eaten and drunk in Shiloh, Hannah rose. Now Eli the priest was sitting on the seat beside the doorpost of the temple of the LORD. She was deeply distressed and prayed to the LORD and wept bitterly. And she vowed a vow and said, "O LORD of hosts, if you will indeed look on the affliction of your servant and remember me and not forget your servant, but will give your servant a son, then I will give him to the LORD all the days of his life" (1 Samuel 1:9-11 ESV).

In her desperation, Hannah ran to the One who could truly help her.

To where are you running in the needs of your parenting journey? To your mom, your friends, your doctor, the specialists? Don't tell me that you don't feel that tug of helplessness and distress. We all do. The question is, where will we run? Parenthood is laced with circumstances that are out of our control, and this can either drive us out of our minds or straight to our knees. For Hannah, her distress took her before the Lord, the only One who opens and closes wombs and human hearts.

Hannah's fervency in prayer looked a lot like drunkenness. "As she kept on praying to the LORD, Eli observed her mouth. Hannah was praying in her heart, and her lips were moving but her voice was not heard. Eli thought she was drunk" (1 Samuel 1:12-13). Hannah kept on praying. Even though it made her look 50 shades of crazy, she sought the only One who had control of her situation. She told Eli, "I was pouring out my soul to the LORD...I have been praying here out of my great anguish and grief" (verses 15-16).

Eli finally understood. What he saw before him was a woman who knew where to run. He said, "Go in peace, and may the God of Israel grant you what you have asked of him" (verse 17). So Hannah went back to her family. The next day they came before the Lord, wor-shipped, and went home. "And the LORD remembered her" (verse 19).

Friend, God never forgot Hannah. And in the quiet, in the times of desperation that we will inevitably have with our children, God never for-gets us. He is present, active, and aware, and He moves to act in response to our desperation poured out in prayer. He pays extra close attention to the times when we drop to our knees and remind Him that He is the only One who can change our situation or the heart of our child.

God gave Hannah the child she longed for, and she kept her vow that she had made to the Lord. This meant that one day she said to her husband, "After the boy is weaned, I will take him and present him before the LORD, and he will live there always" (verse 22).

I can't imagine what this was like. Hannah had finally been given the child her arms ached for, and now she was going to hand him over to be a servant of the Lord, to live in the presence of the Lord, away from her for his entire life. She addressed Eli the priest and said,

> "As surely as you live, I am the woman who stood here beside you praying to the LORD. I prayed for this child, and the LORD has granted me what I asked of him. So now I give him to the LORD. For his whole life he will be given over to the LORD." And he [Samuel] worshiped the LORD there (verses 26-28).

This is the kind of parent I want to be—one who knows where to run, the kind who pours out her heart before the Lord. I want to be the one who hands the children God has given me back to the Lord.

Don't miss the detail that the child worshipped the Lord afterward. In case you don't know the story, Samuel became the final judge of Israel, led the people in repentance, and was very godly. He anointed King Saul and King David and loved the Lord all his days. That's the kind of fruit we are looking for in our families. Let's spend some time on our knees asking God for Him to do that redeeming work in and through our kids.

Father,

I run to You in desperation today, and I'm so grateful that You hear me when I call. I struggle to make prayer for my children the priority it should be in my life. Will You teach me to culti-vate a habit of prayer? Give me faith to believe that You hear and will answer on my behalf. I turn to You as the giver of all good gifts and ask that You would grow in my children a heart that seeks You and an inward nature that is pleasing to You. I ask in the name of Jesus, amen.

Field Note

My son came home from church with a note today. He had it folded in eighths in his back pocket, and I immediately recognized the handwriting as belonging to one of my closest friends and mentors. The letter brought me to tears.

Dear Brendan,

Your name came specifically to mind as I was praying for my grandkids in general. Each day I concentrate on one or more specifically and the rest in general. As your name came up I wondered how I should pray for you this day. The Lord seemed to say, "Pray for Brendan, that his heart will be made ready for the school year ahead." That you might be strong and courageous in your testimony and unyielding in defense of Christ Jesus when tested or taunted. These are the verses that the Spirit gave me for you.

- "The LORD is my light and my salvation; whom shall I fear? The LORD is the strength of my life; of whom shall I be afraid?" (Psalm 27:1 NKJV).

- "He [God] only is my rock and my salvation; He is my defense; I shall not be greatly moved...In God is my salvation and my glory; the rock of my strength, and my refuge, is in God" (Psalm 62:2,7 NKJV).

I know that these verses are probably familiar to you, but perhaps knowing that you came to my mind this morning with these verses to share will be an encouragement to you that others also care and are praying for you as you journey through life and the testings and trials that lay ahead. God will be faithful to see you through as you seek to glorify Him.

Love,
Grandma Hovey

There is no more precious gift than to know that someone else is praying for my son. I'm so grateful to God for filling my life with godly, praying women.*

---

* I know it isn't the norm to have prayer warriors in your life, but it could be. I urge you to head to the Moms in Prayer website at www.MomsInPrayer.org to find all you need to become a strategic prayer warrior with other moms.

9

The Flawed Faithful

Getting Past Our Unworthiness

> Good character is not formed in a week
> or a month. It is created little by little, day
> by day. Protracted and patient effort is
> needed to develop good character.
> ATTRIBUTED TO HERACLITUS

or the last three years I have written and rewritten one word—*faithful*—on my left wrist in permanent marker. The ink has bled off onto more watch bands than I care to count and been washed off in the shower numerous times. Someday, I'd like to make it permanent.

The word *faithful* moves me to tears each time I see it. For the majority of my life I have wondered if I could be faithful to anyone or anything until the last day of the commitment or until death. I wondered if I could possibly hang on when the going got tough, say no when temptation raged, and cross a finish line having lived a life that points to Jesus. This fear that I will be unfaithful has haunted me my entire adult life and has only been magnified within the walls of the church.

My first memory of recognizing my own failure is shortly after I came to know Christ as Savior. I was part of a dynamic youth group with a youth pastor who loved me just as I was. He and his wife set about the task of discipling me with a commitment that I have seen unparalleled in the nearly 25 years since.

From the beginning, Steve and Joanna put a Bible in my hands and taught me that my mind could be renewed and that there was life found within the Bible's pages. One morning a week Steve would sit and answer the questions I had about faith and the Scriptures. Sunday mornings I'd go to Sunday school and hear him teach the Word. Sunday afternoons I'd join a small group of other students, and he'd teach me about leading among my peers. Monday evenings Joanna would meet with me and three to four other girls to study Scripture, helping me make correlations between the Word and my life. And finally, on Wednesday nights, nearly immediately after I came to know Jesus, they let me lead a small group of middle school girls through discussion questions—which quickly turned into me teaching full-blown Bible lessons, complete with outlines. Steve and Joanna were the ones who identified my gift for Bible teaching and affirmed the mysterious urge inside me to spend my life serving the Lord in full-time ministry. Their commitment to me and my growth leaves me speechless with gratitude.

Just as God designed, the more time I spent in the Word, the more I began to recognize all the ways that the lives of those around me did not align with the righteous standard to which God had called His people. First and foremost, however, I realized *I* was a mess. My life did not parallel the life that Jesus seemed to be teaching His followers in the New Testament. The more I read and learned, the more aware I was of the glaring discrepancies in my teenage life, as well as in the lives of those claiming to be Christians around me. It was all so frustrating and discouraging.

I had a predisposition to exaggeration and even outright lying in order to avoid pain and get attention. It felt like the Holy Spirit had turned a spotlight on this character flaw, and at every turn I was aware that it was a habit so deeply ingrained in me that to uproot it would take concentrated effort. I began playing a game with myself to try and see how far into a day I could make it before I lied or exaggerated. Sometimes I fell short by 8:20 a.m., when I would walk in late to class.

I became disgusted with myself and the sin problem that plagued me, and in the beginning, I vowed to make it longer without lying the next day, when I had a clean slate. Little by little, hours stretched into days. Finally, somewhere a few months in, I realized that I didn't need to wait for a new day to have a clean slate—I could simply begin again in the next moment. I would capture that sin in my mind, name it a lie, call it destructive, and ask Jesus to forgive and change me. By the grace of God, that habit in my life was broken, and what developed in its place was a love for the truth.

I wish I could say that sin didn't manifest in other ways, but it did. I found my life riddled with sin patterns and hurts for which I didn't have words. My question, even though I was visibly and undeniably growing, was, "Can I stay the course in my relationship with the Lord?" I realized that God wanted my whole life, and although I desperately wanted to commit to that, I wondered if I had it in me to be faithful to Him. Would I fail Him and walk away?

We don't just think—we *know* that "in all things God works for the good of those who love him" (Romans 8:28). He isn't just working things for good when we have it all together and our character is gleaming bright. We *know* that He works even in our mess-ups and breakdowns and those times when we feel like a failure. His promise is steadfast to those who love Him, the ones He has drawn to Himself. Paul puts it this way:

> Those God foreknew he also predestined to be conformed to the image of his Son... And those he predestined, he also called; those he called, he also justified; those he justified, he also glorified. What, then, shall we say in response to these things? If God is for us, who can be against us? (Romans 8:29-31).

If you and your children are in Christ, saved by faith in Jesus and born again, then you are foreknown, predestined, justified, and glorified.

Before you breathed a breath, you were fully known, handpicked, and died for. God is committed to you and declares you glorified in the heavenly realm as if it has already happened. Friend, this doesn't give us a license to sin; it gives us freedom from the fear that we will mess up and fall beyond His grip. God's commitment to you has nothing to do with your worthiness, and His commitment to your children has nothing to do with their worthiness either. The linchpin in this whole thing is our faith and God's faithfulness.

"It is by grace you have been saved, through faith—and this is not from yourselves, it is the gift of God—not by works, so that no one can boast" (Ephesians 2:8-9). Not even your faith comes from you. It is a gift from God to you. As John MacArthur puts it, "Faith is nothing that we do in our own power or by our own resources. In the first place we do not *have* adequate power or resources. More than that, God would not want us to rely on them even if we had them."[1]

The Lord emphasizes this to us in His own hallway of faith in Hebrews 11. God, through the author of Hebrews, looks back at the saints of old and invites us to consider their portraits and admire the faith of those He esteems. He encourages us to gaze at their stories and to know that their witness should propel us forward in our faith. "Since we are surrounded by such a great cloud of witnesses," the writer begins, gesturing to the portraits hanging on the wall, "let us throw off everything that hinders and the sin that so easily entangles. And let us run with perseverance the race marked out for us, fixing our eyes on Jesus, the pioneer and *perfecter* of faith" (12:1-2, emphasis added).

Who comprises this great cloud of witnesses? Who are the ones meant to spur us on? They are the fathers and mothers of our faith, the ones God boasts over, remembering and celebrating their faithfulness.

"By faith Noah, when warned about things not yet seen, in holy fear built an ark to save his family. By his faith he condemned the world and became heir of the righteousness that is in keeping with faith" (Hebrews 11:7). The story moves on with Abraham, Sarah, Isaac, Jacob, and on and on until we reach the following:

> I do not have time to tell about Gideon, Barak, Samson and Jephthah, about David and Samuel and the prophets, who through faith conquered kingdoms, administered justice, and gained what was promised; who shut the mouths of lions, quenched the fury of the flames, and escaped the edge of the sword; whose weakness was turned to strength; and who became powerful in battle…The world was not worthy of them…These were all commended for their faith (verses 32-34,38-39).

Not one of those men or women was perfect. Not one of them demonstrated flawless faithfulness and character. The people in God's hallway of faith had feet of clay just like us.

Noah got wasted and passed out naked, only to be discovered by his kids. Abraham, the father of our faith, was an outright coward at times and lied out of fear. Sarah laughed at God and gave her servant to her husband to father a child. Isaac the patriarch was a liar. Jacob was a deceiver from his youth, practiced obvious favoritism with his wives and kids, and ended up driving a wedge between his sons. Moses had an anger problem. Gideon became prideful. Barak's courage failed him. Samson's whole recorded life is a mess. And David, the man after God's own heart, was an adulterous and murderous man, as well as a passive and absent parent.

These were the flawed faithful, those whose faith was counted to them as righteousness. When we look back at their stories, we see the glaring failures—but when God retells the stories of their lives, He finds them full of faith in the One who can take our character flaws and drown them through the powerful, purifying blood of Christ.

May we begin to see that the God who drew us to Him in faith, the One who is called Faithful (Revelation 19:11), is the One who will keep us. He is the One who looks past our failures—both the ones we have committed and the ones we will commit—and retells our stories with His eyes fixed on the beauty He finds in our faith.

Our endeavor to raise children of character will fall short if we don't point them to the grace found in Jesus. Let us receive this message with grace, then, and picture the heavenly Father cheering wildly as we move forward with our children in the process of being conformed to the image of Jesus.

> *Father,*
>
> *What extravagant mercy that You call us Your children and count our faith as righteousness. Thank You for Your forgiving nature, and thank You for Jesus. Because You are faithful, we can be too. As I move ahead with my eyes toward discipling my children, be my guide. Show me the moments when their hearts are bent toward instruction and stay my tongue when it would harm them. I seek You again today as the One who knows the path ahead and the One I long to follow. Amen.*

10

Faith When Bullets Fly

An Example in Faith

> "What are we to make of Christ?" There is no question of what we can make of Him, it is entirely a question of what He intends to make of us.
>
> C.S. LEWIS

When the apostle Paul arrived back in Lystra on his second missionary journey, the believers there were talking about a young man who was markedly different from his peers. The book of Acts tells us that believers in the surrounding region were speaking well of a young man named Timothy (16:1-2).

Timothy was born into a mixed family, raised by a Jewish-Christian mother and grandmother while his father was a Greek. Timothy was a disciple of Jesus who showed promise and quite obviously had a heart for ministry. "Paul wanted to take him along on the journey" (verse 3), so Timothy joined the apostle as he "traveled from town to town" (verse 4). While together, they shared the gospel, built up the church, and saw incredible triumphs. Timothy was also there when Paul and Silas were thrown into prison in Philippi and hunted down in Thessalonica, and when Paul had to sail away from Berea for fear of his life (Acts 16–17).

Timothy grew in the Lord and in maturity as they traveled and proclaimed the gospel, and at some point, Paul spurred on Timothy's growth by sending him on trips of his own. Timothy was known for his faithfulness and loyalty to the Word, and Paul trusted him to remain faithful despite the pressures of the people around him. With Paul living as a prisoner and Timothy busy in ministry, they were often apart, but their depth of relationship could not be diminished over the miles. It must have been particularly meaningful for Timothy to hear these words from Paul, his mentor and friend: "Don't let anyone look down on you because you are young, but set an example for the believers in speech, in conduct, in love, in faith and in purity" (1 Timothy 4:12).

Likewise, it is entirely possible for our kids to set an example for believers and the world around them that causes a cultural and spiritual shift. Despite his youth, Timothy lived in such a way that his faith and faithfulness were admired by those much older than him. He was a countercultural disciple who loved the Lord enough to leave home, safety, and his family to share the gospel with men, women, and children who may not have rolled out the welcome mat. This is the kind of change agent our children can become.

We underestimate the possibility that the faith of a child could change us, even though Jesus was crystal clear. "Unless you change and become like little children, you will never enter the kingdom of heaven. Therefore, whoever takes the lowly position of this child is the greatest in the kingdom of heaven. And whoever welcomes one such child in my name welcomes me" (Matthew 18:3-5). Jesus set no minimum age for embracing the kingdom of God, no degree necessary for becoming close to His heart and encouraging others to do the same.

A Frontal Assault

In your hearts revere Christ as Lord. Always be prepared to give an answer to everyone who asks you to give the reason for the hope that you have. But do this with gentleness and respect, keeping a clear conscience, so that those who speak maliciously against your good behavior in Christ may be ashamed of their slander (1 Peter 3:15-16).

There is nothing passive about the attack on our children's faith. The skepticism about and antagonism against faith that used to be reserved for college campuses have now trickled down so that the ideology of godlessness and unbiblical values are now trumpeted in early elementary classrooms. The question is not *if* our children will have questions about their faith, but rather, *when* they will have those questions and how we will respond. Helping our children understand their faith—learning to explain it and also defend it—is a very important part of our job description as parents of the next generation.

One of the character traits that our children will need most is discernment as they face an age in which information is warped and the truth is subject to ceaseless "spin." It can seem easier to clear the path in front of our children, cloistering them in a world carefully screened for anti-faith messaging, than to ready them for the battle. While it is important to protect their minds at tender ages and stages, it is our responsibility to prepare them for the path ahead. We must raise kids who are able to discern the messages around them, and we must prepare them to speak truth when met with antagonism from their peers and worldly messages from the media and teachers.

In one of my new favorite books, *Mama Bear Apologetics*, Hillary Morgan Ferrer raises the need for parents to train kids to be discerning in the things they watch, read, listen to, and see. She explains,

> Discernment is a process, and it doesn't stop at *identifying* the good and bad elements within culture. We must know *why* certain things are considered good or bad...Truth is powerful, and the most potent lies are wrapped in partial truths. If a spoonful of sugar helps the medicine go down, then partial truths help the lies go down...The best Mama Bears teach *their kids how to spot danger on their own* and avoid it![1]

Ferrer and her team have even created an acronym to help mothers know how to do this:

"**R**ecognize the message

"**O**ffer discernment (affirm the good and reject the bad)

"**A**rgue for a healthier approach

"**R**einforce through discussion, discipleship, and prayer...

"The ROAR method is intended to identify a message and analyze its ideas with grace and truth."[2]

This is taking our role as the trainers of our kids seriously. If they can learn to "roar" at the messages bombarding them, we don't have to worry about clearing the path in front of them. We just need to cheer them on and pray them through.

Praying for Boldness and Grit

My oldest son spent his beginning years alternately in a small Christian school and being homeschooled. His first public school experience was in sixth grade, and although we never tried to shelter him, he had been protected from many unbiblical values. He experienced his first true moment of testing with boys he had played baseball with for years. Baseball practice turned into a theology discussion when one boy said, "There's not a God."

My son piped up, "How do you know there isn't a God?"

The others looked at him and said, "Well, how do you know there is one?"

My son replied, "I believe the Bible, and I look at the world around me and see things that God has made."

It has been "game on" since then.

Fortunately, we are finding that rather than crippling him, the questions from science teachers, the conversations at lunch tables, and the barrage of squabbling over sexual identity have sent him running to

Scripture, Christian apologetics resources, and us, his parents. Friend, we have to stop being afraid that our kids will shipwreck their faith while they are in our home and instead convince them that home is the best place for them to ask their questions.

Instead of always praying on the defense, let's pray that God would instill boldness and grit into our kids. They can be the ones who take the heat and ask the hard questions that make room for faith in classrooms, dugouts, and sidelines.

Recently, I came home and found Brendan with his Fortnite headset on, talking to one of his friends about faith. It was not evangelism as I had ever imagined it, but as he sat in one room and I listened in another, I heard him ask, "What questions do you have about faith?" Then, "Do you see that the world is broken? How so? Do you know Jesus came to die for you?" I laughed and cried a little when I heard a few days later that the kid on the other headset had chosen to rededicate his life to Christ. I heard it myself from his mother.

Our kids will use new and different methods to convey the unchanging message of the gospel. My son is testing the waters on how to do this in the most creative ways, and it is fun to watch. I firmly believe that the goal of seeing his peers come to Christ could be a driving force big enough to propel him past the obstacles in front of him.

The Gospel Is Worth It

On my first trip to Haiti, I was unknown to the national pastors of the organization we served. On the night before our group was scheduled to begin a women's conference designed to teach inductive Bible study to women's and children's leaders from five local churches, we were relaxing and making final preparations. It was 105 degrees inside the house where we were staying, and we were all still trying to acclimate to the heat, so I had pulled up a chair on the second-story patio to catch a breeze and look over my notes for the next day. A truck arrived at the gate and beeped its horn, and a group of six to eight men in suits piled out. They were greeted by my host and were quickly invited inside and given something cold to drink. I walked into the room and welcomed them.

The organization we work with has 80 churches throughout the nation of Haiti, but there is a core group of pastors who help oversee their development and growth—and these were the men who had just arrived. We sat on the patio getting to know one another, and they began their examination of my theology. They started with a question about my views on eternal security and went from there. They were wonderful, warm, and smart. The discussion was rich with the purposes of God, and the evening was truly a sacred moment for me. At the end of the night we hugged, and I had their blessing to teach and shepherd their women—a true gift.

We began that conference with 20 incredible female servants of God, me and Jeanna, and one male pastor to supervise our teaching time. Pastor Amazan is a humble man. At the time he was a young 40-year-old Bible teacher, respected by all who knew him. He had been left to babysit us but sat in the back of the classroom and eagerly engaged in our teaching. When our women worshipped, Amazan worshipped; when they needed to work in groups, he eagerly joined in— humbly and without an ounce of pretension. It was a curious time for me, wondering what kind of report he would give to the other Haitian pastors, but he seemed to be enjoying himself and engaging fully. We ended the first day aflame with the gospel, savoring the moments of revelation we had found in the Word and excited for the week ahead.

The next day we submerged ourselves in Romans 2 and came up for air to discuss the ministries the women in the room led. Jeanna and I took notes and listened in awe as the class described to us feeding ministries, Christian schools, evangelistic journeys to the mountains, orphan and widow care programs, prayer ministries, and prison ministries. The list went on and on and was presented in humility, each group of women affirming the others, praising God for what was so clearly happening in our midst.

At the end of our time together, when we seemed to be all wrapped up, one of my Haitian sisters stood and said, "We need to discuss Pastor Amazan's ministry."

He looked up and then humbly bowed his head.

Amazan pastors a church in Cité Soleil, the slums and ghetto of Port-au-Prince, Haiti. The poverty is staggering, but worse is the gang violence, so bad that it makes the south side of Chicago look like a picnic. Gang wars rage, and violence, kidnappings, and brutality were at their peak when Amazan began his trips into the area. It was impossible for him to drive a car there for fear of carjacking, so he would ride a tap-tap bus into the area and walk to the church on foot. He led services and prayer meetings, bringing hope to families crushed by the oppression and violence of the city.

Although Amazan has a beautiful wife and child and lived in an area of relative peace at the time, he accepted a call to Cité Soleil and was often trapped in the church, waiting out shootings and gang wars happening out front, sleeping on the ground for fear of flying bullets.

In the years since my first trip to Haiti, I have been able to visit Amazan's "church." I use the term only to describe the body of Christ represented inside, because the structure itself is a large tent, surrounded by cinder block walls with rebar windows. The danger of stray bullets speeding through the building was inevitable. At one point in the height of the violence, when it was impossible to safely make it into Cité Soleil, Pastor Amazan missed a few Sundays. Some members of the church made the journey by foot to find him.

"Pastor, you cannot leave us. You must return. We need to learn and hear about God. Please come back!" they pleaded with him.

So Amazan, unable to make the journey in by land, took to the sea. Leaving his family and the relative safety of his home, he boarded a small boat to go and shepherd his flock. This was no small feat, because Amazan cannot swim.

The women in our class on my first visit told me that no one would go to that area. No one had the courage to go where Amazan went, and they honored him, prayed for him, and boasted in the Lord about his unwavering faith and commitment to the gospel.

Pastor Amazan laughed when he told me the story of crossing the sea on a boat to get to his people. He confided in me that he was terrified but still moved forward, awaiting the reward on the other side—people who needed hope and truth found in Christ.

Last year, Mike and I were able to go to Pastor Amazan's church in Cité Soleil. It happened to be Amazan's birthday, and when we arrived the humble tent was decorated with paper flowers, and tablecloths were draped around the room in all kinds of colors to make the celebration vibrant. A few women wrote a song about my friend and his voyage on the boat to bring hope to them. We laughed and cried, and about halfway through the hoopla Amazan turned, got down on his knees, and bowed before the Lord. He'd had about enough of celebrating himself and was ready to get to the business of worshipping God. He wanted no recognition; rather, he wanted people to worship Jesus. It's his faith that God brings light to the darkness which is propelling the community into a place of healing.

God may never call our children to risk their lives for the sake of the gospel, but we must pray that they would be willing to do so if He should call. We are looking to raise kids who believe that Jesus is worth it and that the treasure they carry in the gospel can radically change lives. This is countercultural faith. This is the character of an ordinary person whom God can use, one who is willing to take God at His word.

A Lifetime of Faithfulness

The righteous will flourish like a palm tree,
    they will grow like a cedar of Lebanon;
planted in the house of the LORD,
    they will flourish in the courts of our God.
They will still bear fruit in old age,
    they stay fresh and green,
proclaiming, "The LORD is upright;

he is my Rock, and there is no wickedness in him"
(Psalm 92:12-15).

Three years of attending cross-country meets have taught me that
the beginning of the race is important, the pacing in the middle is
important, but the way the runners finish the race determines the vic-
tor. Crossing the finish line of faith requires endurance until the very
end. Our faith is a relationship with a God who is active and engaged
in our lives to the very last breath, when He welcomes us into His
arms. Paul wrote about this burden of finishing well. "I consider my
life worth nothing to me; my only aim is to finish the race and complete the task the Lord Jesus has given me—the task of testifying to the
good news of God's grace" (Acts 20:24).

Let's help our kids see and honor people who finish this life with
faithfulness and endurance. Let's celebrate the accomplishment when
our loved ones and the people in the churches around us die in faith. It
might feel a little morbid, but it's imperative that we discuss not only
living well, but dying well. Our character is most on display when our
pretenses drop to the ground and we prepare to go home. I've watched
one of my best friends finish his race in faith, worshipping until his
last night in the sustaining grace of the Lord. And I've watched Mike's
grandparents make decisions full of faith, pointing to the truth that
matters most in their final years. May it be so in us and our children.

Jesus,

*My heart's desire is that my children will be men and women of
faith. Help me model a life of actively believing that Your way
is the best way and that the gospel is worth my sacrifice. Lord,
cast vision in our lives for a lifetime of faithfulness and help us
run with endurance the race marked out for us, fixing our eyes
on You, the author and perfecter of our faith. Give us boldness
and sensitivity to Your Spirit so we can see the nuances of how
You are working in our midst. Keep us in faith till we rest in
Your arms. I love You. Amen.*

11

Live Loved

Mission Critical

> We please Him most, not by frantically
> trying to make ourselves good, but by
> throwing ourselves into His arms with all
> our imperfections and believing that He
> understands everything—and loves us still.
>
> A.W. TOZER

It was a busy season full of back-to-school activities and lesson prep-ping for the fall women's retreats. In my work hours I was study-ing the books of 1 and 2 Timothy, elbow deep in the apostle Paul's final words to his spiritual son, Timothy. Specifically, I was focusing on this verse: "God gave us a spirit not of fear but of power and love and self-control" (2 Timothy 1:7 ESV).

I have clung to this verse while battling fear, and the chance to study it bit by bit was a fascinating process that changed the way I pray and look at obstacles. Each element—power, love, and self-control—is powerful in its own right. However, I assumed that when I got to the portion about love, I would hit the fast track of understanding. I mean, of course God loves us, right? It's the hallmark of our faith. "For

God so loved the world that he gave his one and only Son, that whoever believes in him shall not perish but have eternal life" (John 3:16). I wondered what I would discover if I dug a little deeper. Would I find some treasure in Greek? Surely, it would bust open something I didn't know.

But nope, the Greek word for love used in 2 Timothy 1:7 is *agapē*, the famous kind of love. The kind associated with divine love. Nothing I hadn't heard or read before.

I realized, much to my dismay, that God giving His love to us felt like a cliché to me—something that was old news, not the good news I'm sure the apostle Paul wanted to sweep over us. I felt ashamed at the realization. I prayed, "Lord, would you make this new to me?"

Within hours I had to admit that although I knew God loved me, I didn't feel very lovable. When I assessed myself, I felt a little unattractive, unorganized, overcommitted, and overwhelmed. When I measured myself, I found myself lacking as a worker, a wife, a mother, and a child of God.

This is when the question dropped right into my heart: "What if I hadn't been loved?"

I knew the answer to this question. I'd seen it lived out in real children. I thought back to my first trip to an orphanage in Kostroma, Russia. When we'd arrived at the orphanage in the land of rolling hills, picturesque valleys, and onion dome churches, we had already been gone from home for a full week. We'd spent that first week working in an orphanage in the Vladimir region of Russia. Despite the sad reality that the children were not tucked into bed each night by parents who loved them in a home of their very own, the staff seemed loving and the kids were engaging and warm. Maybe that's what made the second orphanage in Kostroma seem even colder.

The kids and the situation were so starkly different. The home wasn't as well kept, the resources were scarce, and the staff was more aloof, and as a result the children in this orphanage were much worse off. There was no sparkle in their eyes and very little joy.

The experience undid me. I tucked myself away in an office after listening to the plight of the caregivers, the lack of resources and staff available to work for such minuscule wages. I turned to my friend and sobbed until there were no more tears. The memory still haunts me.

Up close, I've seen how a lack of love early on in a child's life develops within them an inability to receive love later on. This pushes away families and caregivers and makes close, supportive, healthy, nurturing relationships impossible. Not being given love has consequences and leads to all kinds of damaging behavior.

This is also true in our spiritual life. Being loved is not something to be taken for granted; rather, it is integral to who we are becoming as parents and in the lives of our kids. Despite how we feel about ourselves and the way we are treated by the world, we must learn to accept the love of our heavenly Father. A refusal to embrace this love greatly affects our ability to live counterculturally in this broken world and can define us when we are misunderstood, mistreated, and overlooked. We must live loved.

One of the Scripture passages that has been particularly meaningful in my walk with the Lord is found in Isaiah 43. It begins with the Lord speaking tenderly to the people of Israel:

> Do not fear, for I have redeemed you; I have summoned you by name; you are mine. When you pass through the waters, I will be with you; and when you pass through the rivers, they will not sweep over you. When you walk through the fire, you will not be burned; the flames will not set you ablaze. For I am the LORD your God, the Holy One of Israel, your Savior (verses 1-3).

Living loved begins with understanding that God knows us deeply. He knows the number of hairs on our head, a word before it is on our tongue, our predisposition to sin, and the quirks we try to hide. We are fully known and deeply loved, and it is our job as parents to help our children grasp the magnitude of God's love for them as well. It is difficult to do that when we have not accepted this love for ourselves or allowed it to repair the cracks in our hearts that the world and our past have brought.

"Since you are precious and honored in my sight, and because I love you, I will give people in exchange for you" (Isaiah 43:4). Precious, honored, loved. Have you ever had someone take you into their arms and whisper such words over you? Some of us have never experienced this kind of love in the flesh. Some of us missed hearing these words from our parents, and that lack has deeply wounded us. Maybe, just maybe, some of us are still aching to hear, "I want to be with you."

Friend, such words are said over you today, if you will only receive them. You are precious, honored, and loved by God, and this knowledge can set you free to love others wildly. Accepting this love as a parent will empower you to model for your children what it means to live loved.

In Christ, God showed us the extent of His love, sending His Son so we could spend eternity with Him. The Father, quite literally, sent Jesus in exchange for us. "The righteous for the unrighteous" to bring us to Himself (1 Peter 3:18). He sealed us with the precious Holy Spirit, declaring that we are His. Jesus sent His Spirit to believers because He wants to be with us. He has put a deposit on us because if we belong to Him, He is coming back for us.

As Jesus said in the Gospel of John, "I will not leave you as orphans; I will come to you" (John 14:18). I spent the fall teaching this powerful truth, and at one event I asked the women in the audience to turn to one another and say, "You are loved." They of course smiled, laughed, and some even hugged. Then I asked them to turn to each other, make eye contact, and say, "I am loved." Tears every single time. Why? Because we don't feel loved or lovable. In fact, at one event a woman looked right at me and shook her head. I think feeling unloved is part of the human condition.

Even Jesus Needed to Know

There I was in the middle of this study about being loved, and I found myself missing Jesus in my quiet times. I'm a sucker for a good story, and Luke is a fantastic storyteller, so to the Gospel of Luke I went.

I decided to skip over the birth of Christ and the ever-so-brief record of his preteen years and dial in on the beginning of His ministry in Luke 3. At this point, Jesus headed to the Jordan River to be baptized by John the Baptist. The Gospel of Matthew (chapter 3) records the exchange that happened before the baptism, when John the Baptist said—and I'm paraphrasing here—"No way. I need to be baptized by *You*, not vice versa." Jesus, however, assured him that this was part of God's plan, and it had to be done.

> When all the people were being baptized, Jesus was baptized too. And as he was praying, heaven was opened and the Holy Spirit descended on him in bodily form like a dove. And a voice came from heaven: "You are my Son, whom I love; with you I am well pleased" (Luke 3:21-22).

You are mine, and I love You. When the Father broke radio silence with His Son, it was to tell Jesus that He was loved. Jesus had to know. Likewise, it is mission critical to know that *we* are loved by God.

As parents, we must recognize that if it was crucial to Jesus's mission to know that He was loved by God, then it will be even more so in the lives of our children. As we look toward training and equipping them for the path ahead, we must make it a priority to remind them to whom they truly belong—they are God's children, and He loves them.

Securing Identity

This love from God knows no limits. "God demonstrates his own love for us in this: While we were still sinners, Christ died for us" (Romans 5:8). Talk about unconditional love! While we were still hostile to God, rebellious and in sin up to our necks, Christ died for us. This is the breathtaking reality of God's love. Imagine how much fuller and deeper we can know and experience His love once we are His children. This powerful love is expressed in Paul's words:

> In all these things we are more than conquerors through him who loved us. For I am convinced that neither death nor life, neither angels nor demons, neither the present nor the future, nor any powers, neither height nor depth, nor anything else in all creation, will be able to separate us from the love of God that is in Christ Jesus our Lord (Romans 8:37-39).

Our children can be more than conquerors as they live within the fullness of this love. Instead of looking for such love in people, achievements, or their performance, they can live counterculturally, radically loving others out of the well of endless love poured over them.

While our kids will know that they are loved by us and the heavenly Father, the world will assess them by much different standards, ones that are undeniably broken and often unattainable. Our culture places a high value on outward beauty, athletic skill, and the ability to grab others' attention. Our kids live in a system that cruelly measures each aspect of their lives through channels like standardized tests, body mass index, and ratings on social media. If our children do not learn how to live with a secure identity in Christ, they inevitably will be tossed about by the continual stream of input.

Our challenge as parents is to do everything in our power to teach our kids who they are in Christ, ways to wisely navigate their growing world, and how to present their wounds to the Lord. But we must remember that it will be virtually impossible to do this if we ourselves do not live from a place of being loved.

Build in Love

How do we teach our kids to live in the life-changing reality that God unconditionally loves them and that their worth is found in being His child? Let's start here:

Tell them of God's love.

Speak this blessing over their life no matter their age. Look them in the eye, kneel down if they are young or stand on a step if they are a teen or even text them if you have to, and with zero cheese in your voice tell them that God deeply loves them. Add words of your own and bless them, but at the end of the day remind them that all they need is this love freely given to them by the Father. Say to them, "You don't need to earn my love or God's love. It is always yours, no matter what."

From the youngest of ages, I have asked my kids the question, "Who loves you?" The first time I was fully expecting my oldest son to look back at me and say, "You do, Mom." But instead, he looked up at me with his dark brown eyes and said in a voice filled with awe, "God does."

Yup, buddy. That's exactly right. I'm more than happy to play second fiddle.

Tell your kids they are loved when you stare at a report card that is not what you hoped it would be, when they wreck your car, when they break up with their first love, and when someone hurts them deeply. As strong as the temptation is to remind them of all they are good at, the ways they are beautiful, and just how wonderful they really are, establish them in the reality of God's love first. Let the conversation flow from there and roll into the ramifications of being loved no matter what.

Demonstrate your love.

The next time the wheels fall off your child's behavior, tell them you love them. Instead of holding a grudge or giving them the silent treatment, draw them in closer. When everything in you is repelled by your child's actions, stop in that moment and ask God to love that child through you.

"Don't move." Those are the words the Lord whispered to my heart during a particularly hurtful season with one of my kids. It was a reminder for me to remain in the pain and to fellowship as a parent with the heavenly Father, who loves us even when we reject Him.

I have a friend who regularly reminds me that "love covers over a multitude of sins" (1 Peter 4:8). We can and will fail our kids in many ways, but if they know that we love them and delight in them, they will recover. Let's do everything we can to free them up from living with an addiction to our approval by loving them in words and actions despite their performance.

Savor the Word.

Never allow telling the story of the cross of Christ to become dull or boring. Be a celebrator of God's love for your kids by reading the story of the prodigal son found in Luke 15. Memorize verses about God's unending love, starting with 1 John 4:7-12. Make it a project and do it as a family. Pray the Word over your children with thanksgiving, praising God that nothing will separate them from His love. If they are teens, bribe them if needed to get that Scripture into them. I'm banking on it not returning void (Isaiah 55:11)!

Ask them questions.

Ask your children how they know and sense God's love for them. Is it while they are outside in nature, watching the sunrise, or when they read about it in the Bible, or when they hear it in a song? Ask them what they can do because they know God loves them. When you sense the time is right, ask them if they feel loved by God.

Loving in Return

The atmosphere changed when the "Farm Girls" walked into the room. We were in a warm, rural community church filled with salt-of-the-earth, hardworking people. They were conservative and reserved in their demeanor, but it was clear that they had come to learn and have fellowship at our conference. The differences between these regular attendees and the Farm Girls were apparent from the beginning.

The Farm Girls were a joy. They were dressed nicely but had tattoos, piercings, and hair colored in ways not common in rural Illinois. They all walked up and greeted me as I was looking over the lesson and schedule one more time. Their leader followed them in and introduced herself.

"Hi, Lee, we've so been looking forward to today. This is the first time these women have been to a women's conference, and they are so excited. A couple of them aren't saved yet, but the rest of them," she said, gesturing to the group, "have trusted Jesus."

Before this small woman with gorgeous eyes and a beautiful smile sat down, she leaned over and added, "I am a farm program graduate."

I knew what that meant. The Farm Girls are women who have been rescued from sex trafficking, prostitution, and homelessness in Chicago. They've agreed to come to a program in rural Illinois to receive help, counseling, discipleship, career training, and a safe place to live. Many of them don't know the love of God when they enter the program, but there is no denying that they encounter the life-changing love of God while there.

At this particular conference, the times of worship were lively yet reverent. The Farm Girls formed their own musical section, clapping and dancing away. They were engaged when I read the Word and taught about the reason we can live courageously in this generation. I love a group who responds to my words, letting me know that the Spirit is moving and they are tracking with me—and I found my match in these beautiful redeemed women.

Tears streamed down all our cheeks during worship, seeing the power of the gospel in the midst of such a fresh rescue. I could scarcely imagine the trauma these women had endured. During the middle of our second lesson, while reengaging the audience, I had everyone turn to each other and say, "Jesus is the hero of the story." My assistant, Jeanna, later told me that she heard the woman behind her whisper, "Jesus is my hero." It was enough to do us in. This Farm Girl's unabashed love for her Savior was overwhelming.

Capture Your Love for God

It can be difficult to maintain a fresh love for the Father if we don't often remind ourselves of the desperateness of our situation without Him. However, as we discussed at length in chapter 5, God's greatest command to us is to love Him with the totality of who we are—heart, mind, soul, and strength (Deuteronomy 6:5; Mark 12:29-30). If God considers this to be of supreme importance, then we, as parents, must ask ourselves, *How am I teaching my children to love God?*

Our prayer must be for our Father to *capture* their hearts with his love, and for them to respond in love. The best way to do this is to begin modeling love for them. Deuteronomy 6:5-9 paints a picture of how to begin doing this with them:

> Love the LORD your God with all your heart and with all your soul and with all your strength. These commandments that I give you today are to be on your hearts. Impress them on your children. Talk about them when you sit at home and when you walk along the road, when you lie down and when you get up. Tie them as symbols on your hands and bind them on your foreheads. Write them on the doorframes of your houses and on your gates.

Every little moment in our day becomes an opportunity to weave the love of God and our love for Him into our children's lives. There are so many ways to do this that will match your personality, but it begins by wearing your heart on your sleeve with your admiration of the Father. Consider drawing from the following acronym as you allow your children to see your love for the Father.

Celebrate

Acknowledge God's presence

Pray

Thank God

Unpack God's nature

Rehearse God's faithfulness

Engage them

C–Celebrate

Every little thing is cause for praising God's faithfulness. Finding lost keys, getting an A on a test, the holidays, first snow. Let the words roll out of your mouth declaring that God is greatly to be praised. The reality of His unending love should be enough cause for celebration every day, but how great would it be for your family to be known as people who celebrate God in every detail of their lives?

A–Acknowledge God's Presence

Out loud and on purpose, remind your kids that God is present. This means you can talk to Him without making everyone bow their heads and close their eyes, instead acknowledging Him like He is right there with you. Let your kids know when you sense His presence. Let them know if you have struggled to sense it but still know through His Word that He is always with you. And be sure to tell your kids that you enjoy time with the Lord!

P–Pray

When you pray with your kids, it is the perfect time to spend a minute telling the Lord that you love Him. Model a heart for prayer, because that is one place where you and your children can hear from God. Express your love in both your tone and your attitude toward Him in prayer.

T—Thank God

Nothing marks the life of a true Christ follower like gratitude. Not only does gratitude bring praise to God and help your kids see His work, but it actually benefits your children by bringing joy and hope front and center in their lives. It is time to practice what Paul encourages us to do: "Rejoice always, pray continually, give thanks in all circumstances; for this is God's will for you in Christ Jesus" (1 Thessalonians 5:16-18). While the world loses hope and is prone to complaining, a heart of gratitude is one of the clearest demonstrations of love for God and the fruit of the Holy Spirit inside you. Thankfulness is truly countercultural.

U—Unpack God's Nature

Explain the uniqueness of our God among the other gods worshipped around the world. He alone is loving and self-sacrificing toward His children. Celebrate the names and attributes of God with your children and express your love and gratitude for each different aspect of His character. Blast some worship music and dance like a crazy person in the kitchen or play it quietly as they drift off to sleep.

R—Rehearse God's Faithfulness

"We will not hide them from their descendants; we will tell the next generation the praiseworthy deeds of the LORD, his power, and the wonders he has done" (Psalm 78:4). Each generation must hear the ways that the Lord worked before them. Share the stories from Scripture, the deliverance at the Red Sea and the account of David and Goliath, but don't forget to share your own stories of God's faithfulness and provision.

God is always in the process of updating our testimonies. Tell your kids your story in age-appropriate ways and make sure they know how much *you* have needed Jesus and how grateful you are for His love. Mike and I try to rehearse the stories of God's faithfulness with our kids every time we find ourselves needing God to show up in a difficult situation. This practice fills us with hope, faith, and love.

E—Engage Them

Study your kids and look for times when you see sparks of faith in them. When you see those moments, take note. They are what author Gary Thomas calls "sacred pathways."[1] These pathways differ from person to person and child to child. Some people worship with liturgy and candles, some with contemplation and study, while others connect with the Lord best when they spend time outdoors. Maybe the worship that resonates with your kids involves making a Passover meal or learning about the Jewish feasts together, or perhaps there is a spark when they serve people at your local food pantry. Whatever the case, remind them that it is good to love the Lord in lots of ways while also engaging them in the ways that naturally birth love in them for their Lord.

> *Father,*
>
> *What extravagant mercy that You love me the way You do! I could never earn this kind of love. Please open my children's eyes to the richness and depth of Your extravagant, unrelenting love. I pray that this love would drive out the darkness that tries to steal their identity as children of God and rock their security as they live in this world. I ask You to move us to a deeper place of understanding, alerting us by Your Spirit when we begin to drift back to a worldly value system. Your love is everything, Lord. In Jesus's name, amen.*

12

Love Others

Setting an Example in Love

> Resolve to be tender with the young,
> compassionate with the aged, sympathetic
> with the striving, and tolerant of the
> weak and the wrong. Sometime in life
> you will have been all of these.
>
> LLOYD SHEARER

I have only a few possessions in this world to which I am truly attached. One is a porcelain figurine that my mom had in her room when I was growing up, which now sits on a shelf in my bedroom. It's the image of a beautiful woman with the body of a dancer lovingly holding her child in the air. I've always loved the tender look and the moment I imagine happening between them. My mom gave the figurine to me when I brought home my first child. I love it, and though it is probably never going to be in vogue again, it moves me. It serves absolutely no purpose; it just brings me delight. I dust it every so often, when the woman appears gray rather than a silhouette of white.

I also have a hand-forged silver pitcher that Mike and I received when his grandma moved into an assisted living facility after his grandpa went to heaven. For as long as Mike can remember, it sat on the table at every meal, filled with cold water from the tap. So when we were invited to walk through his grandparents' home and take anything sentimental to us, we were delighted to open the kitchen cabinet and find it sitting on the shelf. I love everything about that pitcher. I love the memories that it holds for our family, and I love its functionality. It keeps water cool, always looks sharp, and is virtually indestructible. I use it all the time.

When it comes to the plans God has for us, He has no intention of leaving us on a shelf to be admired and dusted occasionally. He loves us enough to use us over and over again. God does not put a minimum age on usefulness, which means that our children can powerfully serve others as they rest in His hand. In fact, our children can love others with such sincerity and devotion that it seems otherworldly. Our job as parents is to nurture this aspect of their character and help them see that the simple act of loving someone fulfills one of God's greatest expectations of us—"Love your neighbor as yourself" (Matthew 22:39).

Like every other aspect of our character, we turn to the Lord Jesus not only for the definition of the attribute He is calling us to emulate but also for our example of how to live it out. When it comes to loving others, we need to ask, "Whom does God love?" and, "How does He love them?"

God sent Jesus because of His love for the world (John 3:16). God didn't send Jesus because we served His purposes; we didn't. God didn't send Jesus because we were lovely and offered Him love in return; we weren't and we didn't—we nailed Him to a cross. He loved us because He had predetermined our value. Our skin color and socioeconomic position and ability to keep up don't matter when it comes to our worth in God's eyes.

The lineup of those Jesus loved included fishermen, tax collectors, and people with terrible pasts. He was surrounded by sinners and the needy. He didn't give priority to those who could further His ministry with their platform or financial means, and He rebuked those who just played at piety. This kind of love is revolutionary, and it changed history. Jesus's followers loving likewise today can truly be countercultural.

If left to our own devices, our care for others will be in direct proportion to the worth we believe they have in the world. It's natural for humans to value people from whom society can benefit. We honor those with the qualities and characteristics that the world says are desirable. Selfishly, we place greater value on those who can benefit us. But this is in direct conflict with the way Jesus says His followers should behave: "If you love those who love you, what reward will you get? Are not even the tax collectors doing that? And if you greet only your own people, what are you doing more than others? Do not even pagans do that? Be perfect, therefore, as your heavenly Father is perfect" (Matthew 5:46-48).

Our character is revealed in how we interact with the least powerful, least beautiful, and least instrumental people in the room, not the ones easiest to love. Each person has value simply because the image of God has been placed within them. As we think through ways to instill this countercultural value system in our children, let's use the words associated with the character traits we wish to teach. Some of them need a comeback in the worst way. Let's lead that trend.

Politeness

We hear all the time that the next generation lacks manners and common social courtesies, and I find this to be true. Even Christians are failing to train their children to take steps that just a generation ago were nonnegotiable.

Children don't become polite by happenstance. It takes concerted effort from the parents to provide cues until the behavior becomes normative. We don't do this just so our children will be admired by the world or become socially acceptable; rather, we cue our kids so that they will show respect for others immediately, with little thought, expressing value for the individual in front of them. We model this behavior for them, and then we train them to emulate it.

Work on instilling the following polite habits in your children.

Look people in the eye when they speak to you.

This simple practice conveys respect. It says that the person speaking has value. This is easy for some kids to do and brutal for others. I know—I have both types in my home. However, I once heard a woman who is quite shy whisper to her daughter, "Please say hello to Miss Lee." When her daughter didn't immediately obey and continued to cower, my friend turned to her, got right down on her level, and whispered into her ear, "Remember, sweetheart, being shy is another form of selfishness. It's okay to be quiet, but it's not okay to be impolite." You can be sure I tucked that little nugget into my pocket for later use.

Greet people when they arrive.

Our kids can practice this skill by offering a simple, "Hello," when someone slides into the bus seat next to them. Or they can learn to open the door and greet guests with a smile. Recently, Mike went to someone's house, and their child opened the door and said, "Oh, it's you. Why are you here?" This behavior may be permissible for a small child (although it should certainly be corrected), but it is not acceptable from a teenager.

When people enter an environment for the first time and feel uncomfortable, part of our responsibility as Christ followers is to help them understand they have a place with us because they always have a place with Jesus.

Practice hospitality and graciousness.

This is one of those lessons that can be taught to your kids as you model hospitality. When friends come to your house (*when*, not *if*), your family can do little things that convey great value. Have your kids make place tags for the seats at the table or draw a greeting for your guests on a chalkboard. Have them help take coats and talk with them about the kinds of questions they could ask to show interest in the people who are visiting. Remind them that even though some guests are familiar, they should still be treated with the utmost respect. Ask them to give up their normal seat at the table to make others feel comfortable. Hospitality is about paying attention to the little things. I once heard my friend say, "How we treat others is a reflection of who we are, not who they are."

Hold the door open for the person behind you.

It's always shocking to have a door closed in your face. It is polite to pay attention to and value the people who come after you, and it demonstrates deference to yield your right to be first. Your kids can "open doors" in lines and in conversations, and it really is countercultural.

Don't just take my word for it—try it in an airport security line sometime. The simple act of holding the door is actually a great way to show others that they're seen. Require this, enforce it, and make it a habit for your kids so they don't even have to think about it anymore.

Address people by their name and title.

Not only does this habit show people they are known, but it also conveys respect for the role God has given a person in our lives. "Mr." and "Ms." are great for kids addressing all adults, but so are "Aunt Lee" and "Uncle Mike" for when they address adult friends. I know it may be my Southern roots showing, but when my children respond with, "Yes, sir" or "No, ma'am," to their teachers, principal, pastor, friends, and those in authority, they earn instant respect. Why? Because these designations show honor.

Honor

Honor is a foreign word in our world today, so when it shows up it shines like a star. Romans 12:10 (ESV) tells us to "love one another with brotherly affection. Outdo one another in showing honor." To honor someone means to show them respect or esteem, and God's Word tells us to honor other believers, our parents, those in authority over us, and even people whom we find difficult to love.

We can help our children learn to show honor to others by modeling a spirit of honor with our words and actions. Talk your kids through situations where honor is merited—such as addressing veterans, members of the military, police officers, firefighters, and those in public office. Help them learn to honor those who are older than them and to view them as people whose lives matter and whose experiences are valuable and worth hearing.

The news often includes quotes from politicians and reporters that are coarse and lack civility, so when you listen to the news with your kids in earshot, take advantage of the teaching moment by asking them how a reporter or politician could have conveyed honor rather than disrespect. Ask them how they can disagree with someone, even adamantly, but still show respect.

Celebration

One of the ways we can convey value in our self-centered society is to celebrate other people when they win. This is so hard to teach our children. However, how they lose is as important as how they win. We need to help them see that good sportsmanship is a vital aspect of good character. We don't spit into our palms when it is time to shake hands with the winning team; we celebrate with them. And when we don't make first chair in the band, we congratulate the person who beat us.

Losing and not getting our way puts our character on display. Recently, I watched my niece get passed over for an award that I'm sure she really wanted. I could not have been prouder of the way she hugged her friend who got the reward and celebrated her. I know it stung, but what she conveyed with her face and actions was that her feelings were secondary. That is incredible, countercultural maturity.

Compassion

Compassion is one of those words that we use casually and frequently, but its effect on the world is indescribable. Compassion is a blending of two concepts: suffering and sympathy. Baked into the word is the idea that one acknowledges someone else is hurt, injured, weak, downtrodden, humiliated, isolated, separated, or sick.

We see compassion in God's interactions with His people. Let's consider one of Israel's greatest transgressions. After God delivered His people from Egypt with a strong and mighty arm, after plagues and miracles and the parting of the Red Sea and manna from heaven, Israel stood at the foot of Mount Sinai. God called Moses up the the mountain into a cloud full of God's glory for the giving of the law (Exodus 19:17-20; 24:12-18). Moses spent 40 days and 40 nights on that holy mountain in the presence of God and received two tablets of stone containing the law inscribed by God's finger.

It's difficult to imagine being so wrapped up in the glory of God that time melts away. But while Moses had been captivated in God's presence, Israel had already turned their back on God. They fashioned a golden idol in the shape of a calf, fell down before it in worship, and declared this man-made beast their deliverer.

When God shared this devastating news with Moses, Moses pleaded with Him to turn away His righteous anger from the people and remember His promises to Abraham, Isaac, and Jacob to bring their children into a new land. "Then the LORD relented and did not bring on his people the disaster he had threatened" (Exodus 32:14).

Moses headed down the mountain and arrived at camp to singing, dancing, and revelry—not in celebration of the living God Moses had just met with on the mountain, but rather to an image of a cow, hand-shaped by Moses's brother, Aaron. This time it was Moses who became furious. He slammed the tablets to the ground, burned the idol, and forced the people to drink a watery mixture of the ashes. The next day, he returned to the Lord's presence to seek forgiveness for the people, grace undeserved in light of their wayward choices, and the Lord relented from His anger—though not without punishment for some (Exodus 32:33-35).

In the aftermath of this moral failure, God and Moses grew in relationship. Scripture says, "The LORD would speak to Moses face to face, as one speaks to a friend" (33:11). In a moment of boldness, Moses asked God to grant one request: "Show me your glory" (verse 18). This was the Lord's reply: "I will cause all my goodness to pass in front of you, and I will proclaim my name, the LORD, in your presence. I will have mercy on whom I will have mercy, and I will have compassion on whom I will have compassion" (verse 19).

Right there, in the middle of the devastating failure of His chosen people, God revealed that He is a God of compassion. The Hebrew word for "I will have compassion" is related to the word meaning *womb*, revealing to us that God has set His love on His people like a mother sets her love on the child she has birthed.[1] He is stirred with love and compelled to action because of His feelings toward us, even in the midst of our gross failure. The thought is enough to make me weep.

We won't have compassion unless we have a desire for someone's suffering to end, and this character trait we long for is found in our God. "The LORD is gracious and righteous; our God is full of compassion" (Psalm 116:5). "The LORD is gracious and compassionate, slow to anger and rich in love. The LORD is good to all; he has compassion on all he has made" (Psalm 145:8-9). And a personal favorite: "Because of the LORD's great love we are not consumed, for his compassions never fail. They are new every morning; great is your faithfulness" (Lamentations 3:22-23).

It seems the only way we can begin to comprehend God's loving action toward us is within the context of His mercy and grace. Grace and compassion dance together in a waltz that should captivate and mesmerize us. We must consider God's lavish love, His willingness to enter time in the form of Christ Jesus and to go to great lengths to join us in our suffering and ultimately provide a way for it to end. Only then, after this deep consideration, will we begin to sway to the same rhythm of grace and compassion, embracing the depth of God's love and extending it to others.

God on Display

Until Jesus entered time in bodily form, God had mourned the loss of relationship caused by sin. Certainly He understood the catastrophic ramifications that occurred as sin devastated the world—but He had not personally experienced the physical pain involved in living, suffering, and dying as a human. Imagine the reality then that the all-knowing, Almighty One stepped down to truly sympathize with His creation. This is why the incarnation of Jesus matters so much. Jesus stepped into time to come suffer with us and for us.

The writer of Hebrews explains the role of Jesus as our high priest, the One who lives to intercede on our behalf: "We do not have a high priest who is unable to sympathize with our weaknesses, but one who in every respect has been tempted as we are, yet without sin. Let us then with confidence draw near to the throne of grace, that we may receive mercy and find grace to help in time of need" (Hebrews 4:15-16 ESV).

We have Jesus as our helper, but also as our role model. If God's purpose is to conform us "to the image of his Son" (Romans 8:29), then we must fix our eyes on the example He set in Scripture and pattern our lives accordingly—and then teach our kids to do the same.

Throughout Scripture, we see Jesus move toward others in love, and we can do the same. We can image Jesus in the following ways.

See the Need

It's amazing how unobservant we can be. We become so preoccupied with our own lives that we walk right by the suffering of others. For most of us, overlooking others is completely unintentional; we just have busy lives. But we must train ourselves to see and consider the needs of others, or we cannot be moved by compassion.

The Gospels are filled with examples of Jesus noticing the needs of others and being moved with compassion. Seeing leads to action. With some, Jesus saw physical needs, and with others, the needs were spiritual. "When he [Jesus] went ashore he saw a great crowd, and he had compassion on them, because they were like sheep without a shepherd. And he began to teach them many things" (Mark 6:34 ESV).

We can train our children to act compassionately by first praying with them that our eyes would be open to see the needs around us. Then, we begin to help them notice the needs of others. Some of our questions for them could be:

> Is there someone you see who may feel different from others or left out?
>
> Is there someone who might have a physical need and could use special help?
>
> Is there anyone who is sick? Who might be tired? Is someone acting sad?
>
> What is the next thing that person has to do? How can we help make it easier for them or share their load?

Assume the Best

In an environment where people are quick to point fingers, be the first one to assume the best. "[Love] does not dishonor others, it is not self-seeking, it is not easily angered, it keeps no record of wrongs. Love does not delight in evil but rejoices with the truth. It always protects, always trusts, always hopes, always perseveres" (1 Corinthians 13:5-7). This kind of love, the kind that always trusts and always hopes for the best out of someone, can only come when we live by the power of the Spirit.

We can demonstrate this love when someone hurts or inconveniences us by pointing our kids to the truth that people very rarely hurt us on purpose. We can remind them that it is gracious to "overlook an offense" (Proverbs 19:11), and that giving second, third, and fourth chances is just like Jesus.

Offer Forgiveness

We will be hurt. It's what we do with that hurt that will distinguish us from the world. At no point does God say we shouldn't have feelings—that is inevitable. It's what we do with those feelings that is important. Our heavenly Father is always available to hear our needs and the ways our heart has been broken. But then we have a biblical responsibility to offer forgiveness to the other person.

In Matthew 18:22, Jesus said we must forgive "seventy times seven" (NKJV). In other words, over and over again. Of course, we must train our children to protect themselves from all kinds of abuse and to set healthy boundaries, but we also need to teach them that anger leads to bondage. Anger does not produce the righteous life God desires for us (James 1:20), but forgiveness—true, redemptive forgiveness—portrays the gospel each and every time it is offered.

Heavenly Father,

In a world where love has grown cold, our family's countercultural love for others will point people to Jesus. Help me see opportunities to nurture my children's love for others. We want to truly see people and to use our hands to bless and serve others. We need Your Spirit to do this in and through us. Thank You that Your Son gave us the example we can turn to over and over again. We bask in Your love. In Jesus's name, amen.

13

Positive Conduct

Setting an Example in Life

Even small children are known by their actions,
so is their conduct really pure and upright?

PROVERBS 20:11

I just returned from an end-of-the-year school awards assembly. It was difficult to tell who was more relieved to be wrapping things up—the students or the faculty.

I had gone with a handful of other mothers to observe the revelry as teachers gave awards by grade level in each subject and for many extra-curricular activities. Some awards were given for leadership, some for improvement, and still others for academic excellence.

I was struck afresh by how many of the award categories were dominated by students who came from Christian homes. Equally telling was their reception of the awards, as they lacked the self-celebration that we've come to expect from hyped-up kids. In fact, the students I know to be believers who did not receive awards were engaged in positive, respectful support of those around them who did. My heart swelled as I watched them. Even in awkward tween years, the conduct of believers can be markedly different from those around them.

"Conduct" refers to the way someone behaves. In a world that says that winning, notoriety, and popularity matter, children must hear their parents say, "It is how you live out your faith that truly matters." Their worth comes from being children of God, and their calling develops from living out that radical truth before the world. Because we do not take off this identity, the way our children behave in every moment of every day matters. It is altogether right to teach them that when people walk into our home they should know we are believers. When our kids sit in their classrooms, they should be markedly different—and certainly when they swing the bat, run in the touchdown, fall off the beam, or miss the mark. People should be able to tell that we operate from a different system of self-governance than the world.

The disconnect between Christian beliefs and Christian conduct leads the world to call us "hypocrites." While we can't live for people's approval, our righteous behavior gives proof of the things we say we believe. Jesus said, "Let your light shine before others, that they may see your good deeds and glorify your Father in heaven" (Matthew 5:16). We must ask ourselves and our children, "Is the way I am (you are) acting right now pointing to Jesus?"

We have already discussed how our children should be known and recognized for the way they love others. But what about the way they respond to authority, their work ethic, and how they show honor to others? While some aspects of character are difficult to discern, behavior is measurable. It can provide us with warning signs concerning our kids' inward condition. They give us signals based on what they choose to participate in and what they avoid, both alone and with their friends. Those signals must be prayerfully taken to the Lord and considered.

Phone a Friend

One of the bravest steps we can take as a parent is to ask for input from others about the observable character and conduct of our kids. Are there adults in your children's lives whom you trust to be fair and honest with you about what they see in your children? No matter how hard you try, you will have blind spots in your parenting. It is incredibly brave to turn to your kids' teachers, your friends, and even other family members and ask them for feedback about your children's behavior.

Mike and I have attended scores of parent-teacher conferences and have asked questions such as, "What is Gabi like in your class? Is she obedient? Whom does she hang out with? Is she respectful toward you and others?" These questions about all four of our kids have opened the door for teachers to be honest with us. Asking how we can help our kids lead and learn in their classrooms conveys humility.

Have we ever had conflict with a teacher? You bet. In fact, I had a teacher meet us at the door six weeks into the school year and tell me that my son was disagreeable. I had already heard the story that was coming and had wanted to come in ready for a fight, but praise the Lord, I was able to have the wherewithal to simply say, "Oh, tell me about that." What followed was a conversation that contained the other half of what I had heard at home. To be honest, I struggled to sit in a place of humility, and it was a great growing experience for me.

My son continued to have conflict with that teacher for the rest of the school year, and it wasn't one bit fun. In fact, much of what he experienced wasn't fair, but we had the phenomenal opportunity to walk through conflict with him all year, holding him accountable for conveying respect and honor despite his feelings. What an important lesson to learn at age 15! It's one he will apply for the rest of his life.

We recently had the opportunity to talk with some close friends about their child's conduct. We prayed, and after a series of events, we felt like our friends needed to know what we were seeing in their child and the impact it was having on others. It was a huge risk for us, and we did it in prayer and with a little bit of trembling. Their response was a gift. They actually thanked us and told us they would be following up, and a few days later they let us know they'd had some important conversations.

Friend, are you approachable when it comes to your children? Let's take the feedback we receive from others before the Lord and ask Him to sift it for what is right and true.

Newton's Third Law

What a gift it is to shepherd a child's quick and growing mind. I've found my kids are always trying to determine how one thing they are learning correlates with what they have already learned.

When Brendan was five years old, I set him on the kitchen counter to watch me cook dinner. The milk jug was sitting beside him on the counter, and he leaned over and asked, "Does pasteurization come from Louis Pasteur?"

I am sure I looked stunned. I turned slowly and replied, "What do you mean, buddy?"

He pointed to the word *pasteurization*, and then he said, "Louis Pasteur was a scientist. He developed vaccines and stuff."

"Umm, I don't know, but probably."

He was right, the little smarty. At the time he was obsessed with a line of history CDs that introduced him to important people throughout the ages.

Another doozy came not too long ago when discussing the consequences one of Brendan's peers was facing for possessing drug paraphernalia. He turned to me after reporting the incident and said, "That's Newton's third law, Mom."

Say that again?

He continued, "Newton's third law of motion says, 'For every action, there is an equal and opposite reaction.' That means that when we do something, there is always a reaction of the same magnitude."

The fascinating part of this discussion was not science, but the fact that my son was applying it to people's actions and the consequences of those decisions.

Brendan was right: Actions do have consequences. But actions don't always entail equal or opposite reactions in this life. Poor choices often have far deeper consequences than we can imagine, and sometimes good deeds are overlooked or swept aside.

We must pray and help our kids see that each step they take, every decision they make, and even the words they speak propel them toward a future destination. Yes, it is important to teach them the behavior to avoid, but there are at least four positive conduct choices we can teach them that will propel them toward success in life and faith.

Raise Them to Be Teachable

I had no idea what my parents were saying to me when they would cock their heads and mutter, "It must be nice to know everything." By the time I understood that they were being facetious and not flattering, I had nearly grown through my teenage years and out of my lack of humility.

Our kids do need to develop a mind of their own, but one of our jobs when they are young is to teach them to be teachable. According to Dave Kraft,

> To be teachable means that you have the mind-set of a life-long learner. You're consistently open to learning from anyone at any time on any topic. There is no way to escape the fact that being teachable is foundational to spiritual growth and character development in all areas of our walk with the Lord. I have met Christians advanced in age who are still teachable, and I have met young Christians who are not.[1]

Having a teachable spirit does not mean that our children will absorb everything presented to them as truth. Rather, it means that—with discernment—they will be attentive to truth. Consider the following verses.

"The wise of heart will receive commandments, but a babbling fool will come to ruin" (Proverbs 10:8 ESV). Are you, as the parent, modeling a heart of wisdom and teachability?

"The fear of the LORD is the beginning of knowledge, but fools despise wisdom and instruction" (Proverbs 1:7). Do you model the habits of a lifelong learner to your children in all matters of life, especially those of faith?

"A rebuke goes deeper into a man of understanding than a hundred blows into a fool" (Proverbs 17:10 ESV). Are you correctable? How do you respond when confronted or rebuked for your behavior or speech? Do you, as a parent, respond with humility and gratitude toward the one who risked your anger to help you grow?

A home that learns together grows together. Make learning a part of the fabric of your home by modeling teachability and making learning fun. Since all of life is sustained by our loving, wise Creator God, all of life can teach us. Truth is a reflection and characteristic of who God is, so no matter where truth comes from, we should lean into it.

My friend, Hillary, pointed out to me recently that we shouldn't just categorize influences in our lives as Christian or non-Christian, but instead we should teach our kids to chew up anything they learn, digesting the good and spitting out the bad. As Hillary points out in her book, *Mama Bear Apologetics*, discernment is necessary. We can listen to sermons laced with half-truths and read something written from a secular viewpoint, and in both cases we need to discern, chew, and either digest or spit. [2]

I readily admit this is scary as a parent. It *feels* easier to just avoid things that aren't labeled "Christian," but with our children at our side, we need to guide them into truth, model for them the act of seeking wisdom, and then receive it as from the Lord. For our family, this has meant hours at museums learning beside our children, helping point out the areas where we gain understanding or see truth between the lines of the signs we are reading. We've stood in orchards and fields and talked about the growth of plants and the wisdom of God. And we've listened to people with whom we fundamentally disagree in order to hear their heart. This does not mean that the truth of God changes an iota; it simply means we are listening with a heart to learn.

Consider the following as places for growth in your family.

A Teachable Heart	An Unteachable Heart
Listens when others talk	Interrupts or plans its next words
Seeks advice and understanding	Fakes it till it makes it
Takes notes and actively engages in learning	Critiques style of the presentation
Admits its limitations in knowledge and skill	Considers limitations weaknesses
Asks for help	Gives up
Is willing to learn from anyone	Values self and people like itself

True teachability crucifies its pride and leans into truth, wisdom, and growth. For some reason, we are tempted to place greater value on knowledge rather than learning. However, Jesus places great value in the humble process of learning with Him. "Take my yoke upon you and learn from me, for I am gentle and humble in heart, and you will find rest for your souls" (Matthew 11:29). Jesus is "gentle and humble in heart." The King of all puts value on gentleness instead of proving Himself and invites us to come beside Him and learn. This teaching comes from receiving the Word and yielding to the Spirit, but it often presents itself as an opportunity to listen and learn from others.

It is my job to help my children be humble and discerning learners. This process will require them to learn to embrace some character traits that may feel archaic. Helping them become diligent, dignified, and resilient is at the top of my list.

Raise Them to Be Diligent

Scripture is clear that how we work matters. To be diligent is to work with steady determination to see a task accomplished—being attentive to details that matter—and to finish the work in front of you to the best of your ability. It is countercultural to finish a task with excellence. Don't believe me? Talk to your children's teachers, coaches, and employers about the struggles they are facing as they deal with the work ethic among young people.

To make the task of instilling diligence even more difficult, we parents are often the ones taking our kids off the proverbial hook of finishing their work well. Child not being played enough? Quit the team. Project feel too large? Swoop in and rescue. I know this struggle. As a mom of four, I face it every day.

It is unbelievably tempting to remove or ease the struggles our children face, but that doesn't prepare them for the wins, losses, and conflicts they will inevitably face as they walk into adulthood. That's why we need to teach our kids that whatever they do, they must "work at it with all [their] heart, as working for the Lord" (Colossians 3:23). God judges their effort and attitude and takes into account their aptitude and abilities in a way our world can't and won't. Our children's character shines through completing an activity that has stopped being pleasurable.

One of the greatest stories of diligence in Scripture is found in the book of Nehemiah. Nehemiah's God-given mission was a task that was both physical and spiritual in nature, that of rebuilding the broken walls around the city of Jerusalem. At a time when enemies were on all sides, Nehemiah led his people to finish the noble task. He charged the people, " 'The work is extensive and spread out, and we are widely separated from each other along the wall. Wherever you hear the sound of the trumpet, join us there. Our God will fight for us!' So [they] continued the work with half the men holding spears, from the first light of dawn till the stars came out" (Nehemiah 4:19-21). Fifty-two long days after they began, the task was accomplished (6:15).

We should encourage our children to finish what they begin with quality and strength. Is this hard? Absolutely. Sometimes I want my kids to quit as much as they want to quit. But as a parent, no one is in a better position to help them learn the reward of finishing something they thought they could never do.

Just like a coach runs the sidelines of a game, we must come alongside our children and encourage them to persevere in the tasks God has given them. We must help them. As Paul encourages us, "Let us not become weary in doing good, for at the proper time we will reap a harvest if we do not give up" (Galatians 6:9).

Raise Them to Be Dignified

As I have prayed through traits I am asking the Lord to grow in my family, this attribute has been at the top of my list. Dignified people are self-restrained, thoughtful, and honoring of themselves and others. This really is a step beyond self-control; a dignified person exudes a quiet confidence that has nothing to prove, is gracious in opposition and hardship, and has been developed by the fire of trials.

Scripture also calls this trait "nobility." One example is found in the woman of Proverbs 31. "A wife of noble character who can find? She is worth far more than rubies…She is clothed with strength and dignity; she can laugh at the days to come. She speaks with wisdom and faithful instruction is on her tongue" (verses 10,25).

In a world where our leaders fail to use restraint, especially in their words, we must train our eyes to spot dignified behavior in others. Point it out to your children. Ask them who exudes a quiet confidence, godliness, and power under control. Identify for your kids moments in which you see them acting with dignity and nobility. You can say, "I saw you respond respectfully when the referee made a bad call. What a cool response—that's inner strength! Good job, bud."

Raise Them to Be Resilient

Resiliency is a comeback trait shown after a time of failure, suffering, or hardship. It is more than just getting over hardships though; it is flourishing on the other side of difficulty.

In the last year, I've had a particular fascination with the word *resilient* and what it looks like lived out. Military families have asked that I pray for the resiliency of their children after moves and deployments. I've seen it in friends after battling cancer, and I've read books about success after failure. In all of this, I've come to believe that the ability to thrive after sufferings and setbacks is one of the hallmark characteristics of a life filled with the Holy Spirit. Romans 8 says,

> Who shall separate us from the love of Christ? Shall trouble or hardship or persecution or famine or nakedness or danger or sword?…No, in all these things we are more than conquerors through him who loved us. For I am convinced that neither death nor life, neither angels nor demons, neither the present nor the future, nor any powers, neither height nor depth, nor anything else in all creation, will be able to separate us from the love of God that is in Christ Jesus our Lord (verses 35,37-39).

Paul lists these things—suffering, persecution, and hardship—because they are part of the reality of living on this spinning globe. We will face trial and hardship. We will suffer, and we will be brought to the end of ourselves. It is what we do next that counts. It's how we rise after falling that matters. Paul says it best: "I can do all this through him who gives me strength" (Philippians 4:13). Resiliency begins when we find God faithful in the immediacy of the suffering, draw strength from the knowledge that He can be counted on, and believe that He will use this for good in the future.

Worshipping in the Dark

We live in a valley. It's beautiful and has four open acres of trees we planted ourselves. At the side of our yard is a willow tree that is a bit dreamy and somewhat magical. Our kids have spent hours tucked beneath it with branches all around, spinning stories and scenarios that have kept them occupied for hours. We have a large pond behind our house that I have walked around more times than I can count, and we are just up the road from the farmstead on which our family makes a living.

This little patchwork quilt of fields and farms is a great place to raise our family but a terrible spot to connect with the outside world. The cell phone signal is abysmal, and until I added a ten-foot pole to the top of my roof, high-speed internet was impossible. When my parents would come visit, they would drive the half mile up the road and park in an old cemetery to make phone calls. They called it their "office."

You can imagine my frustration when I got the opportunity to begin interviewing people for Moms in Prayer International. This organization I love asked me to talk to awesome people and record the conversations. Without hesitation, I leapt at the opportunity. However, that meant I now needed high-speed internet and could not possibly work without it.

My friends Eric and Stacie opened their home to me. They set up an office in their basement and gave me a house key and permission for my assistant, Jeanna, and me to invade their home. They also afforded me privacy and gave me an external entry point that would allow me to come and go without even laying eyes on their family. I painted the walls of the room, wallpapered a backdrop for videos, and was given a leather couch with scratched-up arms that made the place cozy. It was my first writing office.

I wrote a book proposal in that office and interviewed actors, movie producers, and ministry leaders. For the most part I was tucked away and granted privacy, quiet, and the internet speed that allowed me to record interviews. I knew when Eric and Stacie were home by the smell in the office. The room must have shared a vent with the kitchen, and the smells were incredible. A fresh brewed pot of coffee. Cinnamon sugar doughnut muffins. Something Italian with roasted garlic and onions. On more than one occasion I secured an invite to a noon meal with Stacie while Eric was away at work.

They had purchased this quirky, rambling home that I call "The Manor" with their eye on hospitality for the glory of God. They got a screaming deal on this 1980s home with enough bedrooms on their main level for their family, along with three additional bedrooms, a living area, and an indoor pool on the lower level for others' use. To date, they have taken in a young, broken girl with two children, a family displaced after a layoff, missionaries, and a writer who needed an office. They say yes to hospitality. Yes to God using their home and their lives to impact people for His kingdom.

One day I let us into that office and sank down at my desk to begin the morning. About a half hour later, the beautiful melodies of hymns quietly filled the room. *Eric must be home*, I thought to myself, which was unusual for a weekday. The baby grand piano in the room above my head sang for hours. Not loudly—just enough that we knew Eric was still there. I didn't pay it much thought beyond the absolute gift it was to worship all morning in the privacy of my office, accompanied by the background music played by my friend. Later I locked up and drove home to have lunch with Mike.

"I had the most pleasant morning. Eric was home and played hymns for hours, filling the office with worship. Not a bad spring morning," I told Mike as I made sandwiches.

That's when Mike turned and said, "Oh, Lee, I just got a text this morning from Eric. He was laid off from his job yesterday afternoon."

To this day, I am in awe of what occurred when Eric thought he was all alone in his fear, anger, and brokenness. With a family to support but no job, my godly friend sat at that piano and worshipped. Fingers moving across the keys, he preached the truth to himself that God was on his side, faithful to guide and present in times of trouble. This is the work of a child of God. That day remains the memory I pull up in my mind when hardships come—and boy, do they ever in the life of a believer. It's a built-in part of being a human.

Jesus told us, "In this world you will have trouble. But take heart! I have overcome the world" (John 16:33). What I witnessed that day was Eric taking heart in the Lord. This is the path of resiliency and leaning into God when the trouble comes.

Eric went through a year of unemployment. He spent his days working for friends until he could find another job in his field, only to be laid off again six months later. A few weeks after that, lightning struck their home and burned a third of it, water and smoke damaging the rest. I was in New York City when I got a text from Stacie saying, "Our home is on fire. We are all out safe. Please pray." Mike was already on his way.

Over the last year we have seen our friends glorify God in deep, deep waters. It isn't that they haven't needed help, encouragement, and people to point them to Jesus. They have. But they have walked through fire, quite literally, looking like Jesus. When people look to Stacie and Eric for an explanation of how they are still upright, they are the first to say, "God is good. It's not easy, but God is good." This is the conduct, the outward behavior, that is symptomatic of a life deeply committed to the Savior.

A Place for Suffering

At the end of a long day of speaking and working a booth for Moms in Prayer, I was ready to collapse. I hugged my friends goodbye and thanked them for coming to serve with me, then I packed up the car for the hour-long drive back to the cheap hotel I had booked in Philadelphia, near the airport so I could catch an early flight home.

The day had left me restless in my heart. I had arrived expecting a large event and had found myself teaching a workshop with eight women. Don't get me wrong—eight women can change the world, and each one is valuable. But I found myself weighing the intangible costs of leaving my family of five at home for the weekend in order to come to this event. As I slid into my small rental car, I rehearsed the truths I know with absolute certainty.

Nothing goes to waste in my life, because God works in ways I cannot fathom—and He does not owe it to me to show me how He is working. It is enough to know that He has and will.

The warm spring weather was a welcome respite on that beautiful evening for this Michigan girl, and I breathed a quiet thank-you to the Lord for the sunshine and trees in bloom. Somewhere along the toll road back to the city, I spotted the first sign for Valley Forge. I rehearsed in my mind everything I knew about the place, and my knowledge ended quickly. The only thing I really remembered was that George Washington had been there, which meant it had something to do with the American Revolution.

I have a son who loves United States history, which has grown a deep love for it in me as well. So I pulled off at a rest area that advertised an information booth and went in to see what I could learn about Valley Forge. I discovered it was only a couple miles out of my way, and knowing that I had no appointments to keep—only a flight home in the morning—I decided to go see this historic site.

As I pulled onto the road that would take me to the national historical park, I sighed with relief. The area appeared to be safe, almost park like with families, couples, and bikers at play around me. I rolled down the windows and took the winding road at a lazy pace, enjoying the warm night. I pulled over at every sign I could find, and the story of Valley Forge began to unfold before me.

On September 26, 1777, the British army invaded Philadelphia. It was a strategic move on their part, as the Continental Congress had met there, the Declaration of Independence had been signed there, and liberty seemed to be the air the citizens were breathing. The occupation of the city was difficult for both the enemy and the citizens alike as winter quickly set in and the British soldiers were quartered with the citizens.

A day's march away, the young Continental Army was forming and training under the direction of General George Washington. The general decided to use the plateau field as the place to encamp for the winter of 1777–1778. Men from all 13 original colonies were represented.

As I drove from marker to marker, it finally dawned on me that no battle had been fought at Valley Forge. *What?* I thought that the winter here was key in the Revolutionary War.

As I sat, viewing the breathtaking valley, the pieces came together. "It was here that the Continental Army was desperately against the

ropes—bloody, beaten, battle-weary—and ready to quit."[3] The battle
at Valley Forge was one of suffering, not weapons. About 2,000 men
died from disease in the cold encampment, but all 12,000 suffered for
the freedom of our country.

I read the memorial stones given by the colonies in honor of the
men who suffered at Valley Forge, and I understood. Sometimes God
takes us to painful places, and it will be our endurance, grit, and good
suffering that will win the battle. There would have been no victory for
the United States without the Continental Army's perseverance. The
same must is true in our lives. Nothing reveals the quality of our character like suffering. The place we run to when we ache and our perseverance in clinging to the Lord will determine the amount of ground
taken in the lives of our families and the kingdom of God.

> *Father,*
>
> *You are the anchor that does not give way when our worlds
> rock and sway. You are the One who holds steady, predictable
> and firm, allowing us to rest in You. Thank You that in Christ
> Jesus we find the example we need for living in a culture with-
> out conforming to it. As I guide and direct my children, give
> me eyes to see progress in their lives, those times when they are
> demonstrating character in their conduct, so I can praise and
> encourage them. Where I need to discipline and correct them,
> help me do so in love, always pointing them back to You. In
> Jesus's name, amen.*

14

A Tibetan Mastiff on Its Hind Legs

Setting an Example in Purity

> The discipline of desire is the
> background of character.
> ATTRIBUTED TO JOHN LOCKE

In a time when his people were living by their own moral code—violence, idolatry, and indulgence—Boaz's character spoke for itself. He was a man of standing and wealth, a landowner and a steward of people. I love this description of him: "He was a prominent man of noble character" (Ruth 2:1 CSB). (Oh, that this would be said of our children!) When Boaz arrived on the scene in the book of Ruth, it was the middle of the grain harvest, and his crews were working sunup to sundown to bring in the harvest.

I live in a land like this. We are a farming family. Starting in late September and usually lasting until the beginning of November, we are in the season of harvest. This is a season when every machine runs as often as it can for as long as it can. On our farm, it means a combine tractor operator, a tandem tractor driver pulling a wagon alongside, a semi driver who shuttles the corn, and everyone working with a constant eye on the corn dryer and the bins that hold the harvest. Everything else waits, because there is only so much time when crops will be ready for the picking and before the harvest begins to deteriorate.

For me, the knowledge that this story of redemption in the book of Ruth happened in the middle of busy season speaks to the kind of man Boaz was. Most farmers wouldn't have time to pay attention to the care of a destitute foreigner like Ruth, let alone make provision to rescue her.

When Boaz noticed a stranger leaning over in his field, he asked "Who does that young woman belong to?" (Ruth 2:5). It was a fair question. He was told, "She is the Moabite who came back from Moab with Naomi. She said, 'Please let me glean and gather among the sheaves behind the harvesters.' She came into the field and has remained here from morning till now, except for a short rest in the shelter" (verses 6-7).

Naomi had left with her husband, Elimelek, Boaz's relative, a decade prior when the Lord had brought famine on their land. Now she had returned a broken woman whose husband and two sons had died, accompanied only by a daughter-in-law who loved her. Boaz's heart went out to both of them, and he offered Ruth kindness by telling her to continue gleaning safely from his field and to drink from the water provided by his workers.

> At this, [Ruth] bowed down with her face to the ground. She asked him, "Why have I found such favor in your eyes that you notice me—a foreigner?"
>
> Boaz replied, "I've been told all about what you have done for your mother-in-law since the death of your husband— how you left your father and mother and your homeland and came to live with a people you did not know before. May the LORD repay you for what you have done. May you be richly rewarded by the LORD, the God of Israel, under whose wings you have come to take refuge" (verses 10-12).

Oh, the compassion! Boaz demonstrated deep understanding of Ruth's loss, sacrifice, and faith, and he blessed her. He honored a woman for the depth of her character and shielded and protected her with no agenda of his own.

By the end of the harvest, Ruth had to be tanned from working in the sun, with hands callused from providing for the mother-in-law she loved. At that point, Naomi came to her with a plan: "Wash, put on perfume, and get dressed in your best clothes. Then go down to the threshing floor, but don't let [Boaz] know you are there until he has finished eating and drinking. When he lies down, note the place where he is lying. Then go and uncover his feet and lie down. He will tell you what to do" (Ruth 3:3-4).

Can I interrupt and just say this sounds scandalous? "Ruth, get dressed up, be sure to smell good, and go lie down at the feet of a man who is celebrating the end of the harvest." Honestly, it sounds like a recipe for disaster to me, but notice that Naomi told Ruth to lie at his feet and not at his side. Naomi knew when she heard whose field Ruth had landed in that God was up to something. Of all the men and all the fields, Ruth had been gleaning in the field of a man of God, a man of honor and integrity.

So Ruth followed the directions of her mother-in-law. When Boaz lay down at a corner of the grain pile, she silently lay down at his feet.

"In the middle of the night something startled the man; he turned—and there was a woman lying at his feet!" (Ruth 3:8). Notice the exclamation mark in that verse. Clearly finding Ruth at the end of his makeshift bed startled Boaz.

He asked who she was, and she replied, "I am your servant Ruth... Spread the corner of your garment over me, since you are a guardian-redeemer of our family" (verse 9).

Boaz was not insulted by the request, nor did he feel used. Maybe even greater still, he did not act immorally and take advantage of the woman who came by night, though he certainly could have. For him, the thought of redeeming a woman of virtue was not a hardship but a blessing.

"The LORD bless you, my daughter," he replied. "This kindness is greater than that which you showed earlier: You
have not run after the younger men, whether rich or poor.
And now, my daughter, don't be afraid. I will do for you
all you ask. All the people of my town know that you are a
woman of noble character" (verses 10-11).

Noble character. It's what defined both Ruth and Boaz in the middle of a generation when "everyone did as they saw fit" (Judges 21:25).
I was startled to rediscover the character of Boaz in the context of his
generation, because the times of the judges were known as godless, corrupt, and perverted. Perhaps that is exactly why the Lord recorded this
story of remarkable faith and purity and allowed Boaz and Ruth the
holy privilege of being great-grandparents of King David in the lineage
of Christ (Matthew 1:5-6).

Purity of heart and mind has infinite rewards for our children. We
must call them to live lives of purity—but how we package that message can make or break their understanding of purity and their desire
to comply with its standards.

Be Holy

God's desire for the purity and holiness of His people is so much
more complex than a list of "thou shall nots." The purity God wants
to see imaged in us finds its genesis in who He is and manifests to
the world the change in us. The apostle Peter says it this way: "With
minds that are alert and fully sober, set your hope on the grace to be
brought to you when Jesus Christ is revealed at his coming. As obedient children, do not conform to the evil desires you had when you
lived in ignorance. But just as he who called you is holy, so be holy
in all you do; for it is written: 'Be holy, because I am holy'" (1 Peter
1:13-16).

Our purity of mind and body is a matter of obedience, a call to be
distinct from the evil and perverse generation around us that lives in

ignorance of the promises, provision, and blessing found in a right relationship with God. Peter explains that the way we handle our thoughts and bodies has everything to do with imaging God to a lost and hurting world (see 1 Peter 2:11-12). Our purity not only protects our body, conscience, and family, but it also protects our neighbors as we become living witnesses of the character of God.

When we engage in activities that celebrate darkness or in some way participate with darkness in our life and sexuality, we show a distorted image of God to others. "God is light, and there is no darkness in him at all" (1 John 1:5 NLT). We have the distinct privilege as parents to convey the beautiful picture of health and wholeness found in God's ways to our children who are swimming against the tide of immorality.

Write Their Script Carefully

It was my first trip to the Hearts at Home conference in Peoria, Illinois. It was also the first time I had spoken at length to a group that size, and the environment was electric with excitement and enthusiasm. The women attending the conference were hungry for godly instruction, wisdom, and resources that would shape their homes. They leaned in during workshops, took notes, laughed hard, spilled tears, prayed fervently, and asked questions—many, many, many questions. At the end of a workshop filled with hundreds of women, there would be a line of ladies ready to ask the questions burning on their hearts.

This is what Bible teachers and speakers live for—audiences who engage with the message, are ready to apply it to their circumstances, and ask the questions that have held them back. By the end of the first day, my heart was ablaze, my mind felt a touch mushy, and my feet were begging for slippers.

One evening Jeanna, my assistant and travel companion, and I slid onto chairs at a table in the speakers' dining room, ready to eat dinner.

We sat next to a vivacious, petite woman named Jennifer Degler and her entourage. Jennifer is a force to be reckoned with in the kingdom of God—a counselor, an author, and a teacher who has her finger on the pulse of the family.

At the conference Jennifer's no-nonsense, straight-shooting talk about cultivating a sizzling sex life in the marital relationship had made her the uncontested winner of longest-line award on the convention floor. I teased her about the line at her booth wrapping down the aisle and causing congestion that far surpassed the free massages across the way. She told me that she had grabbed two chairs, set them up facing each other within her booth, and provided quick consultations, answering the questions that these precious women had about their bodies, their husband's bodies, and a thousand other things they had never had the courage to ask about before. They received a listening ear, an unblushing biblical response, and prayer.

The truth is that I have found much the same response from audiences in every environment. In every group there are women who have sexual questions and issues that plague them with nowhere to turn. They have been left to develop their own theology of sexuality, in theory and practice, because the Christian women in their lives when they were growing up were too uncomfortable with their own sexuality to discuss it with their children.

Friend, this cycle of silence within the body of Christ about healthy sexuality must end. In the vacuum of information and teaching left by the church, the world is perpetuating perversion and immorality that will destroy our children. Is this an overstatement? I don't think so. Let's be the first ones to teach our children the truth about their purity, mentally and physically, and to build a healthy script for their minds about sexuality.

Sex is not bad. It is not dirty, and it is not "un-fun." It is a gift to be celebrated and enjoyed in the confines of marriage, and our God offers forgiveness and healing for those of us who have gotten it wrong.

Stop Feeding the Bear

A woman named Su Yun bought what she believed was a Tibetan mastiff puppy while she and her family were on vacation. She was quite impressed by the puppy's large appetite, but it wasn't until two years and more than two hundred pounds later that she realized she had actually brought home an Asiatic black bear. It seems the dead giveaway was when the bear began walking around on two legs instead of four.[1]

I suspect Su Yun is not the only woman to have brought something home to her family only to realize it was a totally different and more dangerous beast than she could have imagined. Perhaps we have tolerated seemingly innocent attitudes in our children that are now a mile wide, or we have purchased a Christmas gift like a television for the kids' room or a cell phone for "our convenience" that has introduced porn into our children's lives.

We must pray that God opens our eyes to the thing masquerading as a puppy that will soon be walking on two legs and demanding meat, and we must begin courageously initiating conversation with our children about sex and purity. Let's be brave enough to talk about the difficult topics so our kids don't have to experience the hard consequences found in living outside God's will.

Following are seven conversations you should have with your children about purity.

1. God always wants what's best and healthiest for us.

Our God is not a cosmic killjoy. In fact, His Word says that in His presence is "fullness of joy" and at His right hand are "pleasures forevermore" (Psalm 16:11 ESV). When it comes to matters of our heart and mind, when God issues a command—like the one to reserve sex for marriage (Hebrews 13:4)—He does so for our benefit. Our children's mental, emotional, and physical health will be protected as they yield to God's boundaries. These boundaries are not there simply for restriction's sake, but rather serve as a guardrail protecting them from the pitfalls of operating outside God's will. "'For I know the plans I have for you,' declares the LORD, 'plans to prosper you and not to harm you, plans to give you hope and a future'" (Jeremiah 29:11).

In our home, conversations about sex outside of marriage are laced with grace and urgency. We have a home that has been touched by the forgiveness found in Christ, and Mike and I are the first to say we wish we had done things differently. Friend, there is grace for our poor choices, but this does not negate our responsibility to teach our children the standard God has for our lives. This means that no matter how deep the pit of sin from which we have been rescued, if we are repentant, we are not disqualified from beginning again. "'Come now, let us settle the matter,' says the LORD. 'Though your sins are like scarlet, they shall be as white as snow; though they are red as crimson, they shall be like wool'" (Isaiah 1:18).

2. We are to be celebrators of marriage.

In a culture that is delaying marriage or skipping it altogether, it is easy to see how devalued a lifelong commitment has become. However, marriage must be presented to our kids in a healthy light, as a sacred relationship between a man and woman ordained by God. Remember with me that marriage was not humanity's idea. The Genesis account regards the creation of man as good, but Adam and Eve together better imaged God to the world (Genesis 2:18). Marriage is a good thing regardless of what the world says, so we must be among those who speak highly of it and celebrate others who live in successful marriages.

We don't need to present marriage as the goal of life, because it isn't. And let's be careful about allowing messages to come into our home that say sex is a basic need, because that's not biblical. However, it is within the sanctity of marriage that sex can and should be enjoyed. So let's let our marriage shine with the light and joy found in the Lord and in the peace found in walking with our spouse in unity of purpose.

3. What we allow into our mind and heart matters.

Our actions follow our thought processes. Jesus said, "What comes out of a person is what defiles them. For it is from within, out of a person's heart, that evil thoughts come—sexual immorality, theft, murder, adultery, greed, malice, deceit, lewdness, envy, slander, arrogance and folly. All these evils come from inside and defile a person" (Mark 7:20-23). This means that where the mind goes, so go we. It makes sense, then, that we should feed righteous thoughts and spend our time thinking about things that, when built upon, will help us choose righteousness. As Paul says, "Whatever is true, whatever is noble, whatever is right, whatever is pure, whatever is lovely, whatever is admirable—if anything is excellent or praiseworthy—think about such things" (Philippians 4:8).

As difficult as it can be to fight against our culture and sometimes even our kids, we are the guardians of our home, and what we allow into our children's minds matters. This should directly impact...

- what we watch on television
- the music we listen to
- the video games we play
- the books, articles, and posts we read
- the conversations we have
- the daydreams and fantasies we allow to grow in our minds

I have a close friend who has learned to identify the times when her mind is the weakest in fighting sinful thoughts. It's when she lies in bed too long in the morning. So for a while we set up an accountability system where she would check in with me when she got up and going. This is proactive behavior.

We must model this defensive mind-set to our kids as well. For a while I had watched a prime-time show that often has implied sexual scenes. I was already watching the show with my hand on the fast-forward button, but one night I felt the Spirit's nudge on my heart. Even on fast-forward, those thoughts were there and brewing. It was a relief to let that go.

My good friend Katie and I were talking recently, and she told me that when she was younger it was acceptable for her to read the Sweet Valley Twins books but not the Sweet Valley High series. When her parents set that limit on her, she rebelled and hid not only the contraband books but also steamy Danielle Steel books. Clearly, this was not an appropriate choice for her young mind. However, she owned that the sin was her own and that her parents had known better.

Ultimately, our kids will learn to make their own choices. I have known people who wear head coverings and conservative religious dress and yet have led lives of immorality, and I have known kids who have not mastered modesty but who have become new creations in Christ. This is a matter of training and trusting our kids—and asking the Lord to work in their hearts to lead them into all righteousness as they trust in Him.

4. Any perversion is a distortion of reality.

Our kids don't have to look for pornography anymore; it comes looking for them. Just a few months ago one of my daughters who loves to read was told that, although there would be no more books in her favorite series, people were writing their own and she could find them online.

When our internet filter flagged pornographic content, I went to my teenage son. He threw his hands up, promising he had not been the one, and asked us to look at the sites that had been visited. I became curious at that point because we have our parameters set tightly.

I soon saw the progression. What had started as my daughter enjoying a fan story of a heroic cat led her to encounter a full-blown rape scene. When approached, my daughter admitted that the content seemed bad but that most of it was over her head and "weird." I nearly threw up when I read the title; someone had lured in kids with the promise of a new story about cats and had introduced violence and perversion.

This is the world we live in, and it is both terrifying and infuriating. It is imperative that we have frank talks with our kids about the dangers of pornography and sex trafficking. Furthermore, we need to tell them that no matter how alluring or safe it may seem to participate in a sexual encounter outside of marriage, there will be consequences that Hollywood just does not depict. We only see a small portion of reality in movies, and it has received a high-gloss finish. The underbelly of this destructive movement has been a cheapening of sex and violent and grievous damage done to men, women, and children.

5. Temptations do not define us.

Staring down opportunities to sin is part of living. Though these situations vary from person to person and in degrees of severity, they are part of the human experience. The apostle Paul explains, "No temptation has overtaken you except what is common to mankind. And God is faithful; he will not let you be tempted beyond what you can bear. But when you are tempted, he will also provide a way out so that you can endure it" (1 Corinthians 10:13).

The question is not *if* our children will be tempted but *when* they will be tempted and *how* they will respond. The writer of Hebrews tells us that Jesus is able to "empathize with our weaknesses," and He "has been tempted in every way, just as we are—yet he did not sin" (Hebrews 4:15). The writer goes on to tell us what to do with the temptations we face: "Let us then approach God's throne of grace with confidence, so that we may receive mercy and find grace to help us in our time of need" (verse 16).

Tell your child:

- Temptation comes with being human; it's what you do when you are tempted that matters. Run to Jesus for mercy, grace, and help.

- Temptations can seize you, and there are some you cannot fight on your own. That is why you need to live in right relationship with the Holy Spirit and seek the help of your parents and friends.
- There is no temptation nor urge Jesus can't relate to and through which He can't help you find a way.
- You parents want to be your allies, and you can go to them with anything.

Then practice your "I'm not surprised" face. We want our kids to run to us with their temptations so together we can run hand in hand to the Lord. We can trust there is nothing that surprises our heavenly Father, and there is no temptation He cannot redeem us from or empower us to walk through. "God has said, 'Never will I leave you; never will I forsake you.' So we say with confidence, 'The Lord is my helper; I will not be afraid'" (Hebrews 13:5-6).

6. The ability to use self-control will define the people we become.

It's high time we have a frank conversation about the destruction we have seen unleashed in the lives of the people we have admired because they have lacked the ability to say no to themselves. This is especially true in the area of purity. Not only is sexual sin rampant, but so is sexual abuse. We must teach both our boys and our girls that they are not victims of their feelings or urges. They can say no to their bodies. They simply must.

7. The need to belong, to be known, to be accepted, to feel affection is valid.

Our kids are not making up these feelings. It is not unusual for them to wish they had someone who would unconditionally love them and faithfully walk beside them. This need can be addressed to a great degree in their family but will be most fully felt in their relationship with the Lord. No person can ever meet this need perfectly, and neither sex nor marriage will ever fill the longing of their hearts. This need inside them is met in Christ, and the tug for more is a call to press in and love Him more.

> *Oh Father,*
>
> *I praise You for being holy and right. Thank You that You are not a God of perversion and that You do not withhold any good thing from those who love You, as Psalm 84:11 says. Help me point to You as not only the standard for purity but also as the One who enables us to walk in purity. Please protect my kids from the attacks and schemes of the enemy and help my children make choices consistent with Your Word and the righteous and pure life You desire for Your children. In Jesus's name I pray, amen.*

15

From the Mouths of Sinners

Setting an Example in Speech

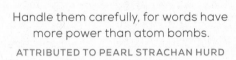

Handle them carefully, for words have
more power than atom bombs.
ATTRIBUTED TO PEARL STRACHAN HURD

We stayed in bed later than usual this morning. It's Saturday, and we had no commitments before 1:00 p.m., which is rare in a house full of kids, so it was nice to roll over and find Mike still home.

He turned to me and asked, "Did I tell you about going to the rental yesterday?" He'd briefly told me that he had been working on replacing a pump in a well for one of the properties the farm manages, but I didn't recall anything that might have him deep in thought first thing in the morning on his day off.

"It was…It was awful," he continued. "I've had to go over there before, but this time the girlfriend pulled up a chair outside while I was working. The kids were outside playing, and one of them was curious about what I was doing. He came over and was asking me questions and talking to me."

He sighed. "But their mom had the foulest mouth I have ever heard. Lee, I'm telling you, almost every other word was an expletive. I've been around some language before on job sites, but this was the worst I have ever heard. Out of a mother, no less. She sat there swearing at her boyfriend, yelling and swearing at her kids. I was so sad, and it made me feel sick as I thought about what it would be like to be raised in the middle of that."

My first thought after Mike told me this was of the report my kids give about the other kids on their school bus. They've always told me that the kids' language is filthy, but it suddenly dawned on me—these aren't just naughty kids running their mouths; they are simply replicating what they've heard at home. Of course they do that—so do my kids. If the steady input children hear at home is noxious, then it should come as no surprise to us when the overflow of their mouths is also poison.

O Lord, keep our hearts, keep our eyes,
keep our feet, and keep our tongues.
ATTRIBUTED TO WILLIAM TIPTAFT

Bits, Ships, and Fire

Many passages in the Bible demonstrate that our words are outrageously powerful and incredibly difficult to restrain. The book of James says, "We all stumble in many ways. Anyone who is never at fault in what they say is perfect, able to keep their whole body in check" (3:2). Did you catch that? Everyone struggles with the words that come out of their mouths. *Everyone.* In fact, this verse says that if you can keep your tongue in check, you have enough discipline to rule your whole body.

I've experienced moments with my kids when I wished with my whole heart I could control what was coming out of their mouths. Once in a grocery store a man with a patched eye walked by us, and my Lexie Beth yelled, "Look, Mom, a pirate!" I said, "He looks like a nice pirate," and did my best to keep on walking before she could say anything else.

I used to break into a sweat wondering what would come flying out of my children's mouths. It was cute when they were little, but if their words were not reined in and trained, they could become unruly.

I often have to stop and ask myself, *Am I in control of what I am saying? What does what I just said reveal about my emotions, motivations, and level of self-control?* I find myself wishing I could stuff words back in that I've let fly. This always brings to mind Proverbs 17:28, which says, "Even fools are thought wise if they keep silent, and discerning if they hold their tongues."

James relates our tongues to a horse's bit, a rudder on a ship, and a spark that can start a wildfire (James 3:3-6). He writes of horses' bits because the trajectory of our life can be changed by the power held in our words—for better and certainly for worse. The quality of our speech and the worth of our words can determine the doors that open and close before us. Likewise, words are like rudders. The tongue is little compared to the size of the body, but what it speaks can define our kids' whole personhood, directing their lives into waves of trouble or toward the calm waters of peacemaking and integrity. And it is obvious to see the way our tongue compares to a spark that starts a wildfire. One only needs to turn on the evening news to see how careless words can impact nations.

We must ask ourselves, *In what direction do I want to head?* Our words will lead us there.

A child of prudent speech can grow into a person of integrity. We see that pattern in the lives of Joseph, Daniel, and Queen Esther in the Bible. Each spoke words that were true and shaped their nations. This is what we are looking to develop in the lives of our kids.

It isn't just our children's positive words that benefit others, but also their words of worship to their God. In fact, the most becoming words on the tongue of a child of God are praise, followed quickly by thanksgiving.

Such words display the inner character of the heart. Rightly, Scripture says, "A good man brings good things out of the good stored up in his heart, and an evil man brings evil things out of the evil stored up in his heart. For the mouth speaks what the heart is full of" (Luke 6:45).

I'm often reminded by the Spirit to make choices with my words that are consistent with grace. I am a woman who has been forgiven much, and it is fitting to remind myself and others that I still need Jesus all the time. When the words we speak are grace filled, hopeful, positive, and good, they reflect to the world a person who understands the gift of Jesus and the reality of His presence in our lives.

We can practice this truth with our kids in the little moments of the day. We can invite them to praise God with their mouths, to point out the things that are lovely and admirable around them. We can ask them to rephrase their unkind words so they become helpful and kind, diligently redoing the conversation until it benefits the listeners, as the Lord requires. The goal is not a heavier "bit" in the mouths of our children; rather, the goal is for our children to operate under our authority in greater and growing freedom and with less and less intervention. We must take the time and mental energy required to fight their grumbling and ingratitude.

We also must steadfastly refuse to allow them to give full vent to their anger toward us and others. "Fools give full vent to their rage, but the wise bring calm in the end" (Proverbs 29:11). Venting anger is wrong, and once it starts it will not stop within the walls of our home. Our kids will carry this negative behavior into their schools, careers, and future relationships.

In our household Mike and I have gotten creative with our discipline in this area, often asking our kids to write out Scriptures they need to revisit, serve the sibling whom they have offended, and face consequences for lack of verbal self-control. It's interesting to see teenagers in time out, but it's effective nonetheless. After all, it is our hope for their lives that when they desire to have the final, mean word, they will instead take a righteous, holy moment to cool off.

Pools of Fresh Water

We were finishing up a long, hot week at camp in Haiti and had just waved goodbye to and hugged the very last carful of women. It's always a huge feeling of accomplishment and relief to cross that finish line with them and graduate another class of women from our Bible school. This day was no exception.

Feeling hot and spent, the entire teaching crew put on swimsuits and headed to the pool. I had been in the pool as often as I could prior to this moment. Have an extra 15 minutes? Jump in the pool. Line too long at lunch? Jump in the pool. Can't feel your lips because you are so hot? Jump in the pool. The pool was out of eyesight of the general camp population, tucked away mostly for use by the camp families.

That last day, all of us had put on swimsuits except Jeanna. She walked out in shorts and a T-shirt, content to spend a while talking to us from the edge. I took one look at her and tackled her into the pool, and she came up sputtering. I thought it would be funny, but Jeanna was shocked to find that the water burned her eyes, tasted bad on her lips, and stayed on her skin long after she left the pool. I've apologized numerous times and promised not to do that again, but my friend still will not get near that pool.

James writes about the shock that happens when people praise God with their mouths and then turn and curse or slander others.

> With the tongue we praise our Lord and Father, and with it we curse human beings, who have been made in God's likeness. Out of the same mouth come praise and cursing. My brothers and sisters, this should not be. Can both fresh water and salt water flow from the same spring? My brothers and sisters, can a fig tree bear olives, or a grapevine bear figs? Neither can a salt spring produce fresh water (James 3:9-12).

It is inconsistent with who we claim to be as children of God to bless God and curse others. Likewise, it is inconsistent to grumble against brothers and sisters, fight on the way to church, or be critical and unkind. As parents, not only do we need to model strict discipline over our own words, but we also need to hold our kids accountable. Destructive words are not consistent with the life of a growing believer and are indicators of a deeper problem that stems from pride, anger, and a judgmental and critical spirit.

We need to present our kids with God's standard: "Do not let any unwholesome talk come out of your mouths, but only what is helpful for building others up according to their needs, that it may benefit those who listen" (Ephesians 4:29). Zip. Zilch. Nada. No unwholesome talk should come out of our mouths. If the words don't nourish and build up others, they don't exit our lips.

Is this hard? Absolutely. Will we talk less? Probably, and that's okay. Sometimes silence is just the ticket to avoiding sin that holds penalty for us and harm for others. On the other hand, this verse also tells us that our words can actually build up, heal, and encourage people.

> Let your speech always be gracious,
> seasoned with salt, so that you may know
> how you ought to answer each person.
> COLOSSIANS 4:6 ESV

It is altogether possible to be ungracious with our words, holding back or refusing to impart forgiveness. This is the exact opposite of imaging God to those around us. Instead, we must learn to persuasively and winsomely turn people back from evil and point them to Christ with our thoughtful and true responses.

> Encourage one another and build each
> other up, just as in fact you are doing.
> 1 THESSALONIANS 5:11

My mom used to tell my little sister and me to edify each other while we were in the middle of an argument. I had no clue what *edify* meant, but we used to yell it at each other as an accusation—"Edify!"

I laugh thinking about how completely ineffective it was on our part, but I know each of us as a parent has been tempted to tell the same to our kids. That's because we know our words have the power to give courage, health, and peace to others.

Mary Slessor served as a missionary in Calabar, Nigeria, in the late nineteenth and early twentieth centuries. When she arrived in Africa from her home in Scotland, this single woman certainly made waves. She quickly learned the language and ways of the people, ultimately befriending a chief.

Mary was known as a peacemaker. She stepped boldly between enraged men and encouraged them toward peace. She proclaimed the truth of the gospel and confronted the practice of infanticide, the abuse of women, witchcraft, and other evils done by the tribal people. "Her fame as a peacemaker soon brought chiefs from other villages to seek her advice. In 1892, the British appointed her as an official vice-consul (similar to a judge) for the area."[1]

The story of Mary Slessor demonstrates the power of a tongue used well. Our children can be peacemakers in their generation, not only confronting the evils of their day but also pointing their peers to the One who can bring them ultimate peace.

Confrontation

Sometimes the word *confrontation* sends shivers up our spine. It is rarely comfortable to raise the topic of someone else's shortcoming. However, part of our responsibility as Christ followers is to help one another walk in consistency with the Word and the ways of God.

Recently, I overheard my son Ryan say to a friend, "Could you please not say that? It's a bad word."

I had been listening to their chattering conversation comparing Beyblades, the newest toy fad at their elementary school. Ryan's friend didn't swear—he just used a coarse phrase—and I laughed a little and leaned in to hear the other child's response.

"Oh, okay."

Two thoughts struck me. One, *That was easy.* Two, *I wonder if my son has that kind of pluck at school? I hope so.*

I love this translation of one of my favorite verses: "You can trust a friend who corrects you, but kisses from an enemy are nothing but lies" (Proverbs 27:6 CEV). I think this means that we need to teach our kids to receive words of correction not as wounds or personal attacks, but as words given in love to help them grow.

I desperately want to be a person who handles confrontation well. I want to be someone who values constructive feedback and listens to the warnings and rebukes of trusted counselors. It's righteous and the best way to do real friendship. We want to be the kind of people to whom others can say, "Ouch. When you said that, it hurt me." We also want to be courageous enough to say the same to them. This is a growth mind-set that has incalculable worth in our life and the lives of our kids. Our children can be the ones who learn to discern the voice of wisdom in the words of others and grow.

Honesty and the Value of Truth

If there is anything missing today in our world, it must be truth. I desperately miss the days when we could take the words spoken to us at face value, although I'm quite certain that the last time I remember that happening for me was in college. Our hearts should break every time we hear the words "political spin" or "fake news." As Christ followers, we must not settle for lies, the native language of the enemy. Jesus said to a group of Jews,

> Why is my language not clear to you? Because you are unable to hear what I say. You belong to your father, the devil, and you want to carry out your father's desires. He was a murderer from the beginning, not holding to the truth, for there is no truth in him. When he lies, he speaks

his native language, for he is a liar and the father of lies (John 8:43-44).

It is not a stretch to say that when we lie, we participate with the enemy in his work. Our Father is the God of truth, and this is why it is paramount that the words that come out of our mouths are true. Otherwise, we once again distort the image of God in front of a watching world.

I'm always amused to watch political speeches when there are real-time streams on Twitter fact checking the statements made. I would hate to stand before a crowd knowing that half of them were waiting for every misspoken word, but what integrity it would require of me if I did.

In our home, there are two offenses that mandate immediate disciplinary action. The first is willful disobedience. If our kids defy a direct order, they receive a consequence without delay—no second chances, no room for debate. As a result, the instances in which our kids have defied us outright have been few and far between. Because of our consistency in this matter, our kids obey authority, and I am so grateful.

The second offense is lying. Under no circumstances may they lie to us, each other, or their friends. If we catch them—we regularly pray that we do—consequences fall hard and swift in age-appropriate ways.

Again, I can count on one hand the number of times our kids have lied in the last five years, but boy, do they remember each of those times. The reason why we stand firm on this is because lying can easily become habitual. If permitted to continue in deceit, kids (and adults) will lie about everything. I know this all too well. However, we try to remind our children often that there are rewards for telling the truth, especially when it is difficult to do so.

- We must teach our kids that the truth sets us free (John 8:32). Telling the truth may result in consequences, but it lets us off the hook of guilt, shame, and the displeasure of the Lord.

- We must teach our kids that trustworthiness is its own reward. We can serve in any position and advance to the top when we can be trusted. Where trustworthiness is not valued, it is not worth the cost to remain in that position or relationship.

- We must teach our kids to look for honesty in their friends and to cut ties with a liar. If someone lies to others, they will lie to you and about you.

- We must teach our kids that they need to take responsibility and tell the truth even when no one else would know they are guilty. I've often said to my children, "I'd rather you disappoint me than lie to me. Disappointment can end, but dishonesty breaks our trust into a thousand little pieces."

On that same trip to Haiti I shared about earlier in the chapter, one of our translators came to us sheepishly with a showerhead in his hands. He looked at our team leader, Becky, and said, "I knocked this showerhead while I was taking a shower this morning, and it fell. I'm so sorry."

Becky assured him that it was okay, that accidents happen, and that she would take care of it. Later, when she went to report the damage, the camp director looked her in the eye and said, "That has never happened before. Things get broken around here all the time, and no one confesses or owns that they were the one who broke something. Wow."

That is the power of integrity in a broken generation. It stands out and points to an inner character that is gleaming with light and truth.

Father,

Thank You that You are the God who tells us the truth. There is no lie or deception found in You, and so we run to You with the confidence that You are good, trustworthy, and true. Please shape our family in this way. Lord, catch our children in lies so that they may become men and women of truth. Build in them a hunger and love for truth. May the words of our mouths and the ways that we use our words call out the best in others. Stop up words that would be destructive. Change us. Start in me, Father. In Jesus's name, amen.

A Parental Response

Stewards, Not Owners

> Though our calling is a serious calling
> which we must work at faithfully, we must
> remember that our diligent efforts will not
> save our children; they may be the means
> God uses to save our children, but we do not
> have the power to change their hearts.
>
> SALLY MICHAEL

Today was one of those days that leaves me scratching my head as a mother. Truly. I spent the day studying compassion, marveling at the wisdom and graciousness of God to choose to set His love on us and pondering his requirement of us to love others in the same way. Like most days, I was part-time writer and part-time mother, and today included an orthodontist appointment, car repairs, grocery shopping, track practice, and driver's training. It had been so pleasant to pause and meditate on this life-changing truth about stepping into the suffering of others when I was interrupted by a heart-stopping text from my son.

"Mom, I need you. I'm in trouble."

It took a couple eternal minutes to get hold of him—and when I did, he answered in sobs.

"I did something really stupid."

This is one of those days when it would be terrific if I could just tell you what happened, and then you would know for certain that the Lord is in the business of constantly updating my list of illustrations through my children. Suffice it to say, today my child did do something stupid. He knew better, and he got caught just the way his father and I constantly pray he will. He will face a consequence that will require some physical labor, and he learned a *huge* lesson about respect and valuing others. As I write, he is sitting behind me, busy with schoolwork.

On the way to pick him up today, I was reminded that the Lord is a God of compassion—and He told us that about Himself on the tail end of the incredible failure of His children (remember Exodus 32–33 and our discussion on compassion in chapter 12). Even there, even right here, God is moved with compassion toward us. Not because of the good we do, but because He has set His love on us.

Praise God for the reminder. Today I had the opportunity to tell my son the same. I had the chance to rebuke, correct, and train him in righteousness (see 2 Timothy 3:16), and all those tasks involved my words. It is such a huge privilege and responsibility as a parent. We hold the power of life and death in our tongues.

That said, good parents have kids that make mistakes—sometimes huge mistakes. Right now, I have one set of friends whose child is serving a lifetime sentence without the possibility of parole and another set of friends whose child is facing trial for sexual assault. Both sets of parents have served the Lord faithfully and raised their families to bring glory to God. Frankly, if either couple wrote a parenting book, I'd read it with anticipation. Yet at this moment I stand heartbroken beside them, asking God to continue His work of redeeming these situations.

Friend, we are not in control of the outcome. If our children end up rocket scientists who serve the Lord on the mission field and happen to stumble upon the cure for cancer while leading an entire village to Christ, we cannot take credit. Likewise, if our children fail catastrophically, that won't be our doing either. Our job is to pray for them, love them, point them to Jesus, and then pray some more.

Red Mug Counseling Fund

On my clothes dryer rests a big, red coffee mug. It is filled with the loose change that often tumbles out of the pockets of pants and coats. I have told my kids for years that the red mug's change is their counseling fund for when they get older. I have embraced the fact that even healthy families have issues they need to work through—and even though Mike and I are doing our best, one day our four kids will probably need help working through parts of their childhood. Why? Because there are no perfect parents, and try as we may, we can't meet their every need.

My goal is no longer perfection, but faithfulness. I desperately desire to be faithful in this job of pointing my kids toward their God. I want to help them know and worship their Savior, aid in shaping their behavior and motivation, and then release them to run after Him no matter where that path leads. It will be my job to wipe away my tears and cheer loudly.

I use the red mug to remind myself that I have feet made of clay. Like every other countercultural parent before me, I will hurt my children. I won't mean to, but I will. And in God's plan there is grace for that, especially when we take a few steps.

Take Appropriate Responsibility of Your Shortcomings

It is not my job to be perfect, but it is my job to be loving, God-centered, and wise. When I fall short of those things, it is time for me to confess my sin to both my heavenly Father and my children when they are impacted.

Rather than verifying our lack of character, sincere repentance and apologies demonstrate our integrity. It takes great inner strength to admit we were wrong and to be humble before our children. Owning our culpability in our choices and sin and their impact on others may be seen by the world as weakness, but within the kingdom of God it is a reminder of the power and strength forgiveness holds. Let's model the fact that the present moment is always the best time to ask for forgiveness. The minute that it crosses our minds to do so, let's act on it. The reason for doing this is simple: We need our kids' forgiveness.

We will say things—hurtful words—they'll remember the rest of their lives. Most of us can recall hurtful words that were spoken to us. I can think of a handful of them that have marked my life. They were offhand remarks that left a scar.

It's not just our words that will hurt our children. At some point we'll miss something that will be very important to them. Hopefully, the "something" we miss will be as simple as a parent-teacher conference or a game where they hit a grand slam. I do not wish to minimize how these instances could hurt our children, but it is also possible we will miss something with more lasting consequences.

We could miss opportunities to discuss sex with them before their "first love," or we could miss signs that they are being bullied. I have loved ones who have overlooked drug addictions and high-risk behavior because their kids just didn't seem like the type, and I have friends whose daughter was active in youth group and top of her class and then announced a surprise pregnancy. We could miss a sin pattern that develops right under our nose, or—God forbid—our children could be abused physically, emotionally, or even sexually without us catching it.

I've come to accept that even as parents who are seeking the Lord and being transformed into the image of God, we will sin against our children. In the middle of the moments when we feel the weight of parental failure, when the enemy comes to accuse us (because he will), we have to know where to run and how to cope. It is in this brokenness, disappointment, and sadness that we run to the cross. Our shortcomings are not the last word in our children's stories. Christ and the power of the cross are the final word, and He is the redeemer of all things.

When we know we have wounded our children, we need to be brave enough to ask for forgiveness from the Lord and them. This makes room for healing to begin relationally and emotionally. God is the rescuer and balm for every relationship. John put it this way: "If we walk in the light, as he is in the light, we have fellowship with one another, and the blood of Jesus, his Son, purifies us from all sin" (1 John 1:7). The knowledge that confession and repentance lead to fellowship and a guilt-free conscience with our children should have us diving for the light. There can be no greater fellowship than the one God brings.

Side with God

It is tempting to lower our standards and justify the weaknesses in our kids. I know this because I usually play the "good cop" in our parenting duo. I want people, even my husband, to view my children through a positive light. It is tempting to try to protect them from the judgment of others, even when that judgment is appropriate. Sometimes this impulse stems from love, and other times it stems from pride in my own heart, a refusal to let them fail. If I'm honest, sometimes my refusal to identify their sin comes from an even deeper fear that I will lose relationship with my children.

I say this now, when our relationships are terrific and my kids are walking with the Lord, but no matter where circumstances find us, our loyalty has to be to the Father, who loves our children more than we do. We must do everything in our power to see the way He sees. We need to stay in constant prayer for His leadership and intervention, asking for eyes to see every situation the way He sees it. We need to own the influence we have in the lives of our children. Finally, we need to love the way God tells us to love, with godliness as our goal but with hearts inclined toward mercy and forgiveness.

Release Control Over the Outcome

Amanda Berry was born into slavery in 1837. Her parents were Samuel and Miriam Berry, both slaves who served on two different properties. Through hard work and the favor of his owner, Samuel was able to buy himself and his family from slavery.

Amanda's father could read and would sit with his family and read the Bible to them at home. When she became a teenager, Amanda worked as a live-in maid and was given the chance to grow in her own education and in matters of faith. Meanwhile, her parents and siblings joined the fight for freedom for other black people held in bondage, with their home becoming one of the main stations in the Underground Railroad. Her parents' example was one of deep love for God, family, and others.

Despite her parents' faithfulness, Amanda became skeptical of religion due to a book she'd read.[1] One day as she was walking with her aunt, her aunt marveled at the beautiful creation of God. Amanda, full of trademark teenage wit and intending to shock her aunt, asked, "How do you know there is a God?"[2]

Amanda's aunt spun on her heel, stamped her foot, and spoke words that Amanda would remember the rest of her days: "Don't you ever speak to me again. Anybody that had as good a Christian mother as you had, and was raised as you have been, to speak so to me. I don't want to talk to you."[3]

And with that shocking rebuke, the Lord moved on Amanda's heart. "How many times I have thanked God for my aunt's help," she wrote. "If she had argued with me I don't believe I should ever have got out of that snare of the devil."[4]

Amanda's aunt is not the only one who has looked at a child and said, "You know enough." Charles Spurgeon's mom did the work of raising her children in the Lord and praying fervently for their salvation. Spurgeon shared in a sermon,

> My mother said to me once, after she had long prayed for
> me, and had come to the conviction that I was hopeless,

"Ah," said she, "my son, if at the last great day you are condemned, remember your mother will say Amen to your
condemnation." That stung me to the quick. Must the
mother that brought me forth and that loved me say,
"Amen" to my being condemned at last?[5]

Reading these words breaks my heart, but they remind me that my
goal is to stand on the other side of eternity and honestly look to the
Lord and say, "Father, I did everything in my power to reach them for
the gospel. I loved, discipled, and trained them. I prayed without ceas-
ing that they would walk with You. They are Yours."

Your Children's Failure Is Not Yours

I just finished talking on the phone with one of the people I love
most on this planet. Her son confessed to using pot and was caught
selling vapes. He is 14 years old. And this was all revealed on Mother's
Day weekend.

The truth is that she is an excellent mother. We laughed and cried
as she said, "I'm doing all the things I know to do. I pray. I spend time
in the Word, and we have family devotions. I have been a stay-at-home
mom, I'm involved, we go to all his sporting events, and we watch his
grades. I know his friends, and he's involved in youth group. I just led
a women's conference for heaven's sake. I'm doing all the things."

She now has her man-child on lockdown. She's done individual
counseling and taken him to talk to his youth pastor, and they are
doing an audit of drug abuse programs. She and her husband are parenting like champs. I wouldn't do anything differently.

I'm reeling with her, and part of me is searching for what she must
have missed—but the truth is that sometimes, despite our best efforts
and our most fervent prayers, our kids make foolish choices. There are
no guarantees, because our children are free agents before the Lord.
And we are too.

That could be terrifying, but in some way it's freeing. You can do everything you know to do and pray fervently, and your kids might still rebel. Still, not one ounce of your diligence in pointing them to the Lord will be wasted. This scripture comes to mind:

> Commit your way to the LORD;
>   trust in him and he will do this:
> He will make your righteous reward shine like the dawn,
>   your vindication like the noonday sun.
> Be still before the LORD
>   and wait patiently for him (Psalm 37:5-7).

Do your best. Pray like it matters—because it does. Praise God when He reveals sin.

He's got this.

Your children are His, friend. They are. We are only caretakers of these little ones for a while, and how they turn out is steadfastly in His hand. The same hand that rescued us is reaching for them. The God that leaves the ninety-nine to find the one lost sheep is searching for our children right now. His love is unstoppable, and He does not rest in His pursuit. Hallelujah!

> *Lord,*
>
> *I know that the way this turns out with my children is not my responsibility alone. I praise You and acknowledge that You are even more invested in how my children turn out than I am. I'm so grateful. I need Your comfort and forgiveness, and I need to be set free from the shame I carry. Give me wisdom on how to point my kids back to You, how to love them in such a way that they always see Jesus in me. I can't do this alone; the burden is too great. I rejoice in the knowledge that You are relentless in Your pursuit of my child and that I can rest in You. I trust You. Amen.*

17

Character Awards

The Final Word

> Talent is a gift, but character is a choice.
> JOHN C. MAXWELL

When my kids were little, they all attended a small, private Christian school. It was the perfect place for them to learn how to read, write, and see God as relevant in every area of learning. It was a worthwhile financial investment, and we loved our time with teachers who did crafts, read lessons, and taught our children songs about the Lord. Academics were a priority, but they were secondary to learning about the nature and character of God and His Son, Jesus. I loved that place.

At the end of each school year, our family would file into the auditorium for graduation and character awards. The ceremony was a celebration of all that the kids had learned and included musical performances. At the end of each grade's presentation, the kids would be awarded a certificate celebrating an aspect of their character. We'd always giggle, because the class talker would receive the "Enthusiasm" award, and the kid whom we would characterize as hardheaded received "Determination."

Of course we laughed, but we also caught a glimmer of who the children were becoming as their teachers blessed the seed of character manifesting in their lives: honesty, kindness, helpfulness, diligence, loyalty.

Kindergarten seems like yesterday as my son climbs into his car and heads off to work. He is definitely the same person, still the boy whose certificate read, "Sincerity"—just significantly bigger.

In the End

It has been a remarkable gift to have all four of Mike's grandparents live into their nineties. Our kids have known and been known by their great-grandparents. On this side of heaven, it is perhaps one of the most precious gifts we could have received. These men and women have invested so deeply in our children's lives, walking beside us to raise them. They housed me as a college student, went on double dates with Mike and me, read books to our children, taught my son English, and called us when the cherries, apples, and rhubarb were ready for picking. They have prayed and loved my husband into the man he has become.

Last year we tucked Grandpa Nienhuis into the arms of the Savior, and at his funeral we rose up and declared him generous, kind, prayerful, and servant hearted.

Today I went to visit Grandma and Grandpa Riley. They just moved into a care facility with Grandma on hospice. I walked in, and Grandpa was sitting in a wheelchair next to Grandma's bed; they were having breakfast together. Grandma, the woman who has invested every ounce of her life into loving Jesus and others, looked up at me and smiled. "Oh, Lee. You're here."

I sat on the edge of her bed and laid my head on her tiny chest and cried. She stroked my hair, and when I sat up, Grandpa grabbed my other hand and said, "The Lord has been so good to us. He opened up a room so we could be here together. We see Him working in so many ways." I sat on that bed and listened to them rehearse the faithfulness of God to the very end.

This time, *I* prayed for *them*. This time, I held Grandma's hands up to my chin and prayed Psalm 91:1 over her: "Grandma, who dwells in the shelter of the Most High, will rest in the shadow of the Almighty." Her voice joined mine in praying our personalized version of verse 2: "I will say of the Lord, 'You are my refuge and my fortress, my God, in whom I trust.'"

She whispered to me, "It is beyond comprehension that we have a God who lets us call Him 'Father.'"

This is what it means to finish well. I don't have to guess what it looks like anymore. I've seen it with my own eyes. Because God is faithful to the very end, we can be too. I have seen it in all four of Mike's grandparents.

It is the Father who will hand out the final character awards: "Trustworthy," "Steadfast," "Virtuous," "True," "Diligent," "Faithful." With all my heart, I pray that the Father will look at us and say, "You remind Me of My Son."

Parents of Prodigals

Dear Friend,

I can't imagine the pain your heart is in right now. I've seen enough close friends with children who have walked away from the Lord to know that this is an ache that is not soothed until your wayward child not only finds his way back to your arms, but back to right relationship in the Father's arms as well. You are not alone in this pain.

In this moment, I want you to know that the training you have done to shape your child's character has not been wasted, and the final story of his or her character is not finished. I see you, and so does the Lord.

May I pray for your child? The him/her thing breaks up every prayer, so will you please put your child's name in the blank as I pray? I mean it for your child with all my heart.

With much love and respect,

lee

Father,

Although we are brokenhearted over the waywardness of this child, we are confident of this, that You who began a good work in _____ will carry it on to completion until the day of Christ Jesus (Philippians 1:6). We believe that You are _____'s refuge and strength and help in trouble (Psalm 46:1). Protect _____ in this moment from the foolish choices and consequences of participating in darkness. Bring conviction and do not allow _____ to walk in willful sin or allow sin to have dominion over this child (Psalm 19:13). Awaken in _____ the truth that has been sown into him/her, and set _____ free from the sin pattern that is entangling him/her. I pray that _____ will love You with all of his/her heart, soul, mind, and strength, putting aside the deeds of darkness and putting on the armor of light (Matthew 22:37; Mark 12:33; Romans 13:12). Father, put a new spirit within _____, and give him/her a tender heart so that he/she will obey You (Ezekiel 11:19-20). We look to the horizon, Lord, for the return of this child. In Jesus's redeeming name, amen.

Recommended Resources

Books and Other Printed Material

Parenting: 14 Gospel Principles That Can Radically Change Your Family by Paul David Tripp

Shepherding a Child's Heart by Tedd Tripp

Wise Words for Moms by Ginger Hubbard

Start with the Heart by Kathy Koch

The Ministry of Motherhood by Sally Clarkson

Women of the Word by Jen Wilkin

Mama Bear Apologetics by Hillary Morgan Ferrer

Raise Them Up by Sally Burke and Cyndie Claypool de Neve

Online Resources

Moms in Prayer International—
MomsinPrayer.org

Jennifer Degler's ministry—
https://www.jenniferdegler.com/service/cwives/

Podcasts

Moms in Prayer Podcast

Risen Motherhood

Notes

Introduction

1. Micah 6:8.

2. Eric Levenson, "Cheat. Bribe. Lie. Here's How the College Admissions Scam Allegedly Worked," *Cable News Network*, March 13, 2019, accessed October 9, 2019. http://www.cnn.com/2019/03/12/us/college-admissions-scheme-how-it-worked.

3. Jacqueline Cutler, "Lies Behind the Laughter, the Truth about America's Dad," *New York Daily News*, April 21, 2019, accessed October 9, 2019, http://www.nydailynews.com/news/national/ny-chasing-cosby-book-20190421-mqiuha5w4je7th7hvhv676pvkq-story.html.

4. Anna Codrea-Rado, "#MeToo Floods Social Media with Stories of Harassment and Assault," *The New York Times*, October 16, 2017, accessed September 10, 2019, http://www.nytimes.com/2017/10/16/technology/metoo-twitter-facebook.html.

Chapter 2: Brick by Brick

Epigraph: C.S. Lewis, *The Great Divorce* (New York: HarperCollins, 2001), 106.

Chapter 3: Welcome to the Revolution

Epigraph: David Platt, *Radical: Taking Back Your Faith from the American Dream* (Colorado Springs, CO: Multnomah, 2010), 7.

1. From *America's Great Revivals* (Bethany House Publishers), noted in "Revival Born in a Prayer Meeting," *Knowing and Doing*, C.S. Lewis Institute, Fall 2004, accessed June 3, 2019, http://www.cslewisinstitute.org/webfm_send/577.

2. "Revival Born."

3. Jonathan Leeman, *The Church and the Surprising Offense of God's Love: Reintroducing the Doctrines of Church Membership and Discipline* (Wheaton, IL: Crossway, 2010), 65.

4. Eugene Myers Harrison, *Blazing the Missionary Trail* (Chicago, IL: Scripture Press, 1949), 48.

5. Harrison, *Blazing the Missionary Trail*, 48.

6. Harrison, *Blazing the Missionary Trail*, 51-52.

7. Harrison, *Blazing the Missionary Trail*, 54-55.

8. *Wikipedia*, s.v. "counterculture," last modified November 10, 2019, accessed June 3, 2019, http://en.wikipedia.org/wiki/Counterculture.

9. *Wikipedia*, s.v. "counterculture."

10. *Vocabulary.com*, s.v. "critical mass," Thinkmap, Inc., 1998-2019, accessed June 3, 2019, http://www.vocabulary.com/dictionary/critical%20mass.

Chapter 4: Get Your Toes Back Where They Belong

1. Charles C. Ryrie, *Basic Theology: A Popular Systematic Guide to Understanding Biblical Truth* (Chicago, IL: Moody, 1999), 252.

2. Jon Acuff, *Finish: Give Yourself the Gift of Done* (New York: Penguin Random House, 2017), 138-139.

3. James A. Swanson, [3567], *A Dictionary of Biblical Languages with Semantic Domains: Greek (New Testament)*, (Oak Harbor, WA: Faithlife, 1997), Logos electronic edition.

Chapter 5: Severe Discipleship

1. Jason DeRouchie, "Love God with Your Everything," *Desiring God*, October 10, 2013, http://www.desiringgod.org/articles/love-god-with-your-everything.

2. John MacArthur, *The MacArthur New Testament Commentary: Matthew 16–23* (Chicago, IL: Moody, 1988), 339.

3. MacArthur, *MacArthur New Testament Commentary*, 339.

4. Pope Francis, "Homily of His Holiness Pope Francis: St. Peter's Square, Sunday, 14 October 2018," *The Holy See*, accessed November 18, 2019, http://w2.vatican.va/content/francesco/en/homilies/2018/documents/papa-francesco_20181014_omelia-canonizzazione.html.

Chapter 7: Moral Compass

1. J.I. Packer, *A Quest for Godliness* (Wheaton, IL: Crossway, 2010), 110.

2. John MacArthur, *The MacArthur New Testament Commentary: Romans 1–8* (Chicago, IL: Moody, 1991), 141.

Chapter 9: The Flawed Faithful

1. John MacArthur, *The MacArthur New Testament Commentary: Ephesians* (Chicago, IL: Moody, 1986), 60-61.

Chapter 10: Faith When Bullets Fly

Epigraph: C.S. Lewis, "What Are We to Make of Jesus Christ?" in *God in the Dock*, ed. Walter Hooper (Grand Rapids, MI: William B. Eerdmans, 2014), 170.

1. Hillary Morgan Ferrer, *Mama Bear Apologetics: Empowering Your Kids to Challenge Cultural Lies* (Eugene, OR: Harvest House, 2019), 53-54.

2. Ferrer, *Mama Bear Apologetics*, 54.

Chapter 11: Live Loved

1. Gary Thomas, *Sacred Pathways: Discover Your Soul's Path to God* (Grand Rapids, MI: Zondervan, 2010).

Chapter 12: Love Others

1. Francis Brown, S.R. Driver, and Charles Briggs, [BDB 933.1] *The Abridged Brown-Driver-Briggs Hebrew-English Lexicon of the Old Testament*, ed. Richard Whitaker (New York: Houghton, Mifflin and Company, 1906), Logos electronic edition.

Chapter 13: Positive Conduct

1. Dave Kraft, "Leadership," *ESV Men's Devotional Bible* (Wheaton, IL: Crossway, 2015), e-book.

2. Ferrer, *Mama Bear Apologetics*, 50-52.

3. "The British in Philadelphia: Part 3 of 3," *USHistory.org*, accessed June 12, 2019, http://www.ushistory.org/march/phila/valleyforge.htm.

Chapter 14: A Tibetan Mastiff on Its Hind Legs

1. Colin Drury, "Pet Dog Raised by Chinese Family for Two Years Turns Out to Be a Black Bear," *The Independent*, May 14, 2018, http://www.independent.co.uk/news/world/asia/pet-dog-black-bear-china-family-grow-kunming-yunnan-stand-endangered-species-a8350451.html.

Chapter 15: From the Mouths of Sinners

1. Dave and Neta Jackson, *Hero Tales: A Family Treasury of True Stories from the Lives of Christian Heroes*, vol. 1 (Minneapolis, MN: Bethany House, 1996), 130.

Chapter 16: A Parental Response

Epigraph: Sally Michael, *Mothers: Disciplers of the Next Generations* (Mendota Heights, MN: Truth78, 2013), 20.

1. Ruth A. Tucker, *Extraordinary Women of Christian History: What We Can Learn from Their Struggles and Triumphs* (Grand Rapids, MI: Baker, 2016), 130-132.

2. Amanda Smith, *The Story of the Lord's Dealings with Mrs. Amanda Smith the Colored Evangelist: An Autobiography* (Chicago, IL: Meyer and Brother, 1893), 30.

3. Smith, *Story of the Lord's Dealings*, 30.

4. Smith, *Story of the Lord's Dealings*, 30.

5. C.H. Spurgeon, "The Chaff Driven Away: A Sermon," no. 280, *The New Park Street Pulpit* (October 23, 1859): http://www.spurgeon.org/resource-library/sermons/the-chaff-driven-away#flipbook.

Acknowledgments

Heavenly Father—You are worthy of a lifetime of my best thoughts and worship. I fully intend to spend my life pursuing You and finding You faithful. I love you.

Mike—This one cost us, didn't it, Love? Thank you for believing this is *our* ministry. I'm so proud to be your wife and grateful to parent beside you. You are a good man, a great father, a humble man of God. Love you forever.

Brendan—You are extraordinary, humble, and brave. When I asked if I could tell our story, you said, "If it helps people grow, and you tell them I've changed." Bubbs, not only are you different, but your story is also helping other parents and kids find Jesus. Thank you. Keep leaning into Jesus. He is always faithful. Semper Fortis, Son.

Gabriella, LexieBeth, and Ryan—Being your mom is a gift. Dad and I see your faith steps and the way you are choosing to say yes to Jesus even when it's costly. We are cheering you on with all our hearts. I love you a million gillions.

Jeanna—You are the best sidekick a girl could ask for. There are no words to express my gratitude for staying in it with me and for believing that somehow, someway, God in us will do it. I love serving Jesus with you.

The Big Sisters—Framily. I love you.

To our families—I continue to be grateful to be a Ford-Tutor-Riley-Nienhuis. Each of you is a gift. I love you.

My Moms in Prayer Family—Thank you for loving me and for teaching me to pray. I am so glad to be yours. Our mission sets my heart ablaze. I love chasing after Jesus with you.

Our Grace Adventures Family—First my ministry "home" and now my home, home. I'm so grateful to be neighbors and to be joining you in the trenches of reaching families. Thank you.

My pastors and elders—I've come to learn most women in ministry don't have the unwavering support of their home church. You not only support, you also pray, share books, take phone calls, brainstorm, and hold us up. You are deeply esteemed and loved.

Katie—The Martha to my Mary. Overwhelming gratitude and love.

Kate, Shannon, and Brenda—I love being in the trenches with you. Thank you for praying.

Hart MIP Girls—Friendship and praying with you is a great joy.

Kathleen Kerr—Forever friends. I'm so glad the Lord brought us together. It's an honor to be one of your authors and to be sharpened by you.

Betty Fletcher—You are the kindest word whittler. So grateful.

Harvest House Team—Deepest thanks for letting me be on your team and for standing like a lighthouse in this generation.

About the Author

Lee Nienhuis is an author and passionate Bible teacher. She is the communications specialist for Moms in Prayer International and the host of the Moms in Prayer Podcast.

Lee's writing and speaking have been featured on *Focus on the Family* broadcast and magazine; *True Woman* blog; Proverbs 31, Hearts at Home, Iron Sharpens Iron conferences; GEMS Girls Clubs; and American Heritage Girls. She shares a dynamic vision for the next generation of Christ followers.

Countercultural Parenting is her second book with Harvest House. Her first book is *Brave Mom, Brave Kids*. Lee and her farmer-husband, Mike, have four kids and live in West Michigan.

For more information about Lee, her books, and writing/speaking ministry, visit www.LeeNienhuis.com.

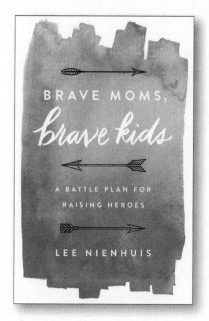

Hey, Mama

This world feels as if it's spinning faster every day. As the darkness has crept in, your brave prayers may have given way to fearful pleas that your kids would experience God's kingdom—in a safe and comfortable way.

This generation *needs* heroes of the faith and your child can be one of them, but that will require you to be strong and BRAVE. You and I must call out the bold Christ followers within our children and help them face the unknown future with divine confidence.

Brave Moms, Brave Kids is an equipping tool that will help you...

- **identify** the qualities present in true greatness
- **reject** "mommy fears" and replace them with immovable truth
- **learn** strategies for praying for and training your children more effectively
- **develop** seven key lessons we must teach our children to live for Jesus

Courage starts with you, Mama. If you're going to raise a hero, you must become a hero—because brave kids need brave moms. Let's do this, together.

Love, Lee